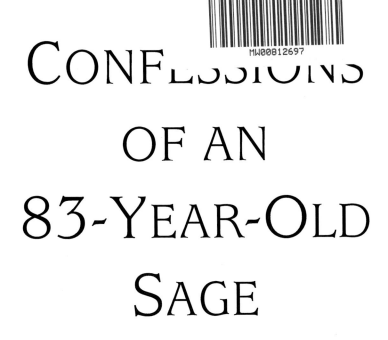

CONFESSIONS

OF AN

83-YEAR-OLD

SAGE

The GLAD-SAD-MAD of Life

Helene Hadsell

Delight in all the GLAD-SAD-MAD that life has to offer.

Carolyn

Updated by
Carolyn Wilman

7290268 Canada Inc.
(416) 356-1116
info@ideamajesty.com

For details on quantity orders, contact the publisher at orders@ideamajesty.com

Hadsell, Helene
    Confessions of an 83-Year-Old Sage
    The GLAD-SAD-MAD of Life
Second Edition of Confessions of an 83-Year-Old Sage
    Body, Mind & Spirit 1. Inspiration & Personal Growth 2. Mysticism.
    Psychology 1. Metaphysics.
    I. Hadsell, Helene. Confessions of an 83-Year-Old Sage: The GLAD-SAD-MAD of Life

Paperback ISBN: 978-0-9939254-9-8
eBook ISBN: 978-1-7773194-0-3

Cover design by Mark Lobo of doze!gfx.

DEDICATION

This book is dedicated to my sons Dike and Chris, the students who encouraged me to 'tell it' the way I perceived and experienced life so that my grandchildren and great-grandchildren will know what a magical journey I had.

To Helene and all the great teachers that came before me, not only did they make my life better, but they also changed countless lives.

Helene Hadsell
June 1, 1924—October 30, 2010

AFFIRMATION

Helene liked to repeat a simple phrase whenever she lectured, wrote, or counseled people:

"Let me be a channel to help people help themselves."

As she isn't here to state this phrase, may each one of us reading these words affirm her prayer.

TABLE OF CONTENTS

FOREWORD

Life is a daring adventure or nothing.
Helen Keller

Helene Hadsell's life was an adventure that she wanted to share with everyone. It began when she was six years old and had her first encounter with spirit. As Helene grew, so did her connection to the Universe, along with her studies into other realms and mysticism. Her path crossed with many teachers familiar to us all, and she enjoyed a 30-year friendship with José Silva.

Helene's desire to teach others about different dimensions, spirit guides, and all the adventures that life has to offer inspired her to write this book. Now, with this republished volume, you can join Helene each morning at breakfast as she taps into her intuition and chooses an engrossing tale to tell us all.

Helene was a marvel and never stopped writing. It took her over a year to complete this book. If you are an avid reader of Helene's work, you may also notice a few stories that sound familiar. Helene pulled stories from *In Contact With Other Realms* to put into this new volume, as it was out of print at that time. Plus, she was also replicating Dr. Joseph Murphy's teaching technique of repeating stories to reinforce the lesson. Helene also included new stories, some of which had never been told before.

In 2008 I was lucky enough to spend four days with this vibrant, remarkable teacher. It was on that trip Helene gifted me a copy of this book. It was during that same visit that she also suggested I start teaching others what she had been sharing for decades. Helene didn't see herself continuing to teach due to her advancing age. Yet, she didn't want her message to pass with her. A decade passed before I finally stopped holding the gauntlet she had given me and started republishing her works. I've experienced nothing but blessings from doing so, and I hope you feel the same by learning from Helene.

It is important that I maintain the integrity of Helene's work, and therefore I have only made minor adjustments in this edition. This book has been reformatted for current publishing methods (Amazon, Kindle, Kobo, Google Books, and Apple Books). I've added notes where required, as well as a Recommended Reading section at the end, so you may continue to learn and grow. I've also made it easy for you to distinguish Helene's words from mine. All of Helene's words are in Arial font. All of my words are in Times Roman font.

Just like Helene, it is my hope you take her wisdom to heart and create your own **DARING ADVENTURE** in life.

Carolyn Wilman
Marketer, Author, Teacher
www.IdeaMajesty.com

INTRODUCTION

An odyssey. A journey into other realms in search of answers. That describes Helene Daschel Hadsell's life. She has lived with the philosophy that 'life is either an exciting adventure, or it's nothing.'

This remarkable woman sprang from what one might consider unremarkable beginnings. Born in the small town of Aberdeen, South Dakota, Helene was the second child of George and Katherine Daschel. George was of Russian descent, Catherine of German, and they lived in the midst of the Aberdeen German/Catholic community.

Perhaps even at a very young age, Helene realized that she was different. At least at the age of five, when she had her first experience at journeying amongst those other realms, she knew, even if she didn't understand, that she had a gift few people had been given.

A sought-after speaker, Helene has given seminars on the spirit connection, mind control, positive thinking throughout the United States, but Europe and South America as well.

She is an author with several bestselling books to her credit, among them the treasured *The Name It & Claim It Game* outlining how she has, through positive action, won almost every contest she's ever entered, including winning a beautiful new home in Irving, Texas.

And finally, she is undertaken to let the world know and to help them understand the wonderful journey she has had through her ability to visit with those other spiritual realms.

It all began in Aberdeen, and it hasn't ended yet, but it's best to let Helene tell her own story.

It's a gift to you and all those throughout the world who like to share her very own special odyssey, her journey in search of answers.

Shirley McKee
Professional Writer

CONFESSIONS OF AN 83-YEAR-OLD SAGE

REFLECTIONS

The mind is like a well
Springing forth ETERNAL WISDOM
To refresh and replenish the human spirit.

It's June 1, 2006, and it's my 82nd birthday. After I got out of bed at 8:30 a.m., I cautiously walked into the kitchen and made two cups of hazelnut decaf in my mini Mr. Coffee Maker. I filled my coffee mug, grabbed a banana, and headed for the living room to my comfortable recliner.

My favorite place in the living room is by the window because I can see the birds at the feeders that hang outside. This morning they came flying straight up to the rungs, fighting for space at the feeding ports, pecking at each other, wings humming and breast burnt white in the sun, feed spilling from their beaks. They fly off and come back, semi-hovering, nine, ten, eleven birds, some in trees nearby, not singing exactly, but what's the word? Twitter? Peep? Squawk? They attack each other on the rungs or scramble in midair. I never get bored watching.

After I finish eating the banana, I sigh and look down at my lap at the backs of my hands, fingers stretching. Looking and thinking, I recall moments with people I know, not moments exactly, but times. I slipped into one of my melancholy moods as I studied the point where my knuckles shine bloodless from the pressure of my grip on the coffee mug. That's when the idea surfaced, or was it a small voice in my head that prompted me to start writing my story? I even have the title: *Confessions of an 82-Year-Old Sage.* I've visualized the cover so; clearly, it seems like I'm holding it.

"No time like the present to get started," I say out loud. It's time to turn on my laptop, and that's exactly what I do.

I propped up my feet and let my body melt into a comfortable position. My mind will do the talking as my fingers do the walking.

Maybe I better clue you in on how I go about writing. I sit and wait for past experiences to surface. I never know what will come to mind, so

I don't expect a proper time sequence. Be prepared, for all keep reminding you that I'm 82-years-old.

NO! I'm not senile, so cut me a little slack.

My first thought is, "Don't ever think that you've used up all of your pleasures. Keep expecting and recognizing more as they unfold, no matter what age you are."

I pause and look up. My eyes are drawn to a dust bunny under the couch. Whenever I notice something that needs to be done around here, I am reminded of the sign my husband wrote up and tacked in the back entry hall many years ago.

My family and friends use that entrance when they come to visit. What prompted him to make the sign was the day that Tanya, our 10-year-old granddaughter, was visiting. Her mother, my daughter-in-law, is an immaculate housekeeper. My husband called her a nitpicker. Anyway, Tanya came to me and asked, "Grandma, don't you ever dust?"

After my husband heard that remark, he grinned and did something about it. This is the sign:

WELCOME
if you see something that bothers you—like mowing, dusting, sweeping, washing, or anything else "feel free" to do something about it OTHERWISE you can wait until you are 80 years old and see if it still bothers you.

WELCOME

If you see something that bothers you, like overgrown grass, dust bunnies, the dirty carpet, soiled dishes, and filmy windows, or anything else, FEEL FREE to do something about it. Otherwise, you can wait until you're 80-years-old and see if it still bothers you.

Now I have an excuse. My interests don't shrink with age, although my ability to do things does!

My recliner is surrounded by a clutter of books, notebooks, a box of NIPS candy, mail, and yesterday's newspaper that I haven't read. I read three books at a time and always keep a notebook handy to jot down every phrase, thought, analogy, or profound bit of wisdom that I find worth remembering. I have a thick loose-leaf book where I file the information according to subject. When writing an article or letter, I review the material, and in my own words, I build a better original description of what I want to convey. It's one of my 'compulsive disorders' that gives me great pleasure

Are you ready to follow me as my thoughts jump from place to person? The only explanation I have been able to figure out is; a thought surfaces by association—like the dust bunny that triggered the incident that prompted me to tell you about my husband's sign. Some thoughts seem to appear out of the blue—like this one.

Nursing home residents include everyone from club women to family cast-offs. Now, why would I think of that? Is it the fear of one day living there? It better not be. I've discussed the issue with my two sons. My exact words were, "If you guys ever put me in a nursing home, I'll come back in the next lifetime and shoot you." I'll get **MAD** just thinking about it. My choice is to LIVE, not just EXIST.

Let's get off that subject for now. Perhaps in memory will surface that will put me in a **GLAD** mood.

I'm usually good-natured, but I can get disgusted with people at times. Let me put it this way I love everybody, but sometimes I don't like what they do or say.

The nearer I get to the end of my life, the less I mind the thought of death. It's just a change—for the better.

This entire lifetime I've looked at life as a DARING ADVENTURE, and DEATH is my next GREAT ADVENTURE. I welcome it.

Oh! Oh! I'm shifting gears again as I'm now led to share with you how visualization is not only a FUNtastic tool; it can help solve problems by giving you ideas and advice to project energy if healing is the issue.

It was early July 1992. After sixty years of being in this physical body, the discomfort in my abdomen became a nuisance. I tried to ignore it because I had lost confidence in the medical profession do the number of unpleasant past experiences, but I knew I could no longer ignore the constant pain. Sensing that there could be something seriously wrong with my elimination process. I reluctantly had to admit that it needed attention. Still, I kept postponing going to the doctor.

Earlier that year, I was invited to be a key speaker for the Silva Mind Control Convention to be held in Laredo, Texas, on August 11th of that year. I look forward to touching base with the many friends I met in line while in the lecture circuit.

One morning after an uncomfortable night, I sat in my recliner, sipping tea, when I had to face reality and admit that I needed help. I had a visitor from the Twilight Zone. (No, not the television show. For me, the Twilight Zone is the fourth dimension, where a number of people, including myself, can see and communicate with spirit beings.) I believe that some of the visitors we see are thought-forms we create, and some are apparitions that come to guide us in our time of need.

The visitor who appeared was small in stature and looked to be about sixty years of age. His deeply lined high forehead and slanted eyes indicated he must be Asian. He wore a loose white knee-length coat over his white pants, which led me to believe he was a doctor. It was his eyes that fascinated me. They were like summer lightning one minute and clear soft blue the next. I sensed wisdom, intelligence, and understanding behind those eyes.

Your body needs attention on the physical level. You have been neglecting it too long, and it is now time for you to take care of it, he communicated as he stood in front of me for less than a minute before he disappeared.

I felt comfortable that he was there to help me. I made an appointment immediately, and that afternoon I sat in the waiting room at the doctor's office. After an examination and hearing my symptoms, the doctor recommended a sonogram and X-rays.

"Let's get this over with as soon as possible," I said impatiently.

The following morning I took a battery of tests as an outpatient. Two days later, I was back in the doctor's office to hear the results.

The doctor had the X-rays displayed on a lighted panel when I arrived. He pointed to a mass in my bladder that was causing the problem and recommended surgery.

"I will not be able to do the surgery because it might be cancer. I feel an oncologist should do the surgery, and I could recommend several top surgeons in Dallas. I can make an appointment for you today," he offered.

"But I can't have cancer. I never learned to develop it," I said as my heart thumped uncomfortably.

He stared at me for a second, probably baffled at my response, and explained, "I've consulted with two of my colleagues. They agree that surgery is required."

Before I left the office, his nurse made the appointment for me to see the oncologist.

That night as I lay in bed reviewing what I was about to face, the doctor from the Twilight Zone reappeared.

No! There is no cancer. It is an infection around a tumor that is blocking your organs. It must be removed. You will be fine, and I recommend that you approach this experience with **humor**.

"You gotta' be kidding," I said out loud when I heard that suggestion.

I am not joking. It is a much better approach than fear, and I will be by your side to help you through this learning experience, he assured me.

Two days later, I sat in the waiting room of the oncologist. After we met, he led me to his examination room, where my X-rays were displayed. He'd circled the tumor and said it definitely needed to be removed

"Can you tell—is it a boy or a girl?" I asked in a serious tone. I wish I had a camera to snap a picture of his expression. It was truly a KODAK moment.

"Mrs. Hadsell. I understand you're over sixty years of age, and it's unlikely that you could be pregnant," he patiently explained as his eyes narrowed. He looked like he was trying to decide if I was for real or only playing dumb.

I kept up the serious tone and said, "I guess you don't read the National Enquirer. Space aliens have been coming down impregnating women for quite some time now."

He turned and looked at me. He didn't sigh or roll his eyes; he didn't have to. He knew how to deliver a stare.

Walking to his desk, he picked up my medical file, looked at it briefly, then asked, "Mrs. Hadsell have you had a brain scan?"

"Why, no, why would you ask that?"

"Because what you were about to undertake is serious," he said as his face clouded with concern.

"OK, let's make a deal. You be serious, and I'll be silly. Lighten up. Lighten up. I'm joking," I said, trying to put him at ease.

He was only casually amused as he ushered me into his office so we could discuss the next steps to be taken

"I'll make the arrangements, and we can schedule the surgery for next Friday," he said after looking at the appointment calendar on his desk. "You need to fill out a consent form to have the blood transfusion," to explain to hand me the paper to sign.

"Why is that necessary?"

"It's a precautionary measure. I found that patients in your age group bleed more during major surgery, and I want to be prepared."

"I'm glad you called that to my attention. I will stop the bleeding, so that should prove to be no problem."

"You will what...?" he muttered as he gave me another KODAK moment, you know—the I-can't-believe-what-I-just-heard look.

I sense that my last remark needed an explanation.

"It's mind over matter technique. I've used it in the past. It is quite effective, and it's one less complication you will have to be concerned about," I assured him. "Here, give me the form. I'll sign it if it pleases you."

He watched as I signed my name.

"I want to have the surgery Monday," I added as I felt this doctor would be the one to help heal his body.

"That's impossible. I'll need to reserve the operating room, contact the anesthetist and another doctor to prepare."

"Well then, don't just sit there. Get on the phone and make it happen. I want to get this over with as soon as possible, so I can get on with my life."

Too startled by my request to offer any objection, he got on the phone, and within fifteen minutes, all the arrangements were made. (I must explain I have another compulsive disorder: I'm pushy.)

I was to spend the night in a hotel annex to the hospital, so I could report Monday morning at 7:00 a.m. for surgery. Yes, I was scared. I would be lying if I said I wasn't, but for some reason, I KNEW it was the thing to do and that it would be OK.

After arriving home that afternoon, I headed for my recliner to review the day's activities. My Twilight Zone doctor was sitting in a chair in front of me, ready to help me sort things out.

Now let's review what is in store for you. You will have sufficiently recovered and will speak at the convention. There will be some discomfort, which you must accept, as it is just an unpleasant experience one has to bear while in a physical body. You'll be able to handle it sufficiently with the techniques you witnessed during your stay in Russia. Remember, everything is energy. Energy comes in pulsations. When you give it negative energy with fear, it becomes almost unbearable. When you repeat 'healing-healing-healing' instead of 'hurting-hurting-hurting' the energy changes and feels like waves of soothing soft strokes, and the body heals more rapidly. Review all of this information so you can prepare yourself.

I have what some people might consider to be a hang-up. I chose not to tell or discuss my physical problems with family or friends because I know how the mind works. Just the word cancer frightens people. The first thing they think about is how many people they know that have, or had, cancer and how they suffered. The next thing they do, is think of me, and I pick up their thoughts and fears, and I have to deal with not only my own thoughts but with theirs. So… the only person who knew I was going in for surgery was my husband because he, too, knows how the mind works, and I could count on his positive support.

One of my friends that I met at the lecture circuit summed it up this way. "Don't tell anyone about your problems—fifty percent could care less, and the other fifty percent are glad you got 'em."

NO! That's not Christian thinking, but it is thought-provoking.

Monday morning, after checking into the hospital, I was put into a small room where I was slipped into a gown, was helped onto a gurney, and given a shot. Five hours later, I opened my eyes and saw two doctors, the anesthetist and my husband standing around my bed.

"We want to know how you stop the bleeding?" the anesthetist asked.

"She talks to her body and tells it how to behave," my husband answered, relieved that I would be all right. I was immediately aware of all the tubes attached to my body. My one goal was to get out of that place as soon as possible.

"When you feel pain, just press this button and medicate yourself with drugs." The doctor pointed to a bag hanging on a pole by the bed. I never pressed the button. When I was aware of discomfort, I mentally changed the pain pulsations to healing waves of energy.

The following morning when the doctor came by to check me, he read my chart and shook the plastic drug bag. He then asked the nurse if they'd hooked up another bag and didn't record it. She replied they hadn't.

"Don't you have any pain?" the doctor asked with concern.

"Yes, I do, but I want to clear my system of drugs. I don't want to depend on drugs."

"You're probably one of those people who have a high pain tolerance," he rationalized.

I didn't tell him that my doctor from the Twilight Zone was giving me better advice than he was. I was out of the hospital in three days and presented my speech at the convention two weeks later.

Funny thing, the doctor from the Twilight Zone only appears when I ask for advice about a physical, mental, or emotional challenge.

If my experience sounds far-fetched, I suggest you read Rebecca Latimer's book *You're Not Old Until You're Ninety*. She, too, had a doctor from the other dimension and also used visualization to speed up the healing process.

GRATEFUL

I turned on the news to have a break while I fix myself a cup of green tea. The following report got my attention.

In Indianapolis, Indiana, there is a television program called, *Never Too Late*. The purpose is to encourage senior citizens to send in the request for something they want to do before they die. This morning they interviewed an 86-year-old woman who drove a race car at 120mph on the speedway track in Indiana. She explained that it was something she had always wanted to experience, even as a child. Then there was a 90-year-old man who wanted to stand in a cornfield and pick an ear of corn. Another woman wanted to feel the fur of a tiger. She was taken to the zoo so she could experience it. One woman, confined to her room in a nursing home, wanted a typewriter so she could type instead of write her poetry longhand.

Three cheers for the person that thought up the *Never Too Late* opportunity for seniors and did something about it.

At this time in my life, I can only think of one thing that I would like to see happen. I want to stay around long enough to finish my confession stories, put them in a book and see the book displayed at Barnes & Noble bookstores.

NOTE: As Helene self-published this book, it was never in Barnes & Noble. However, she saw fit to have me carry on her legacy, and now her books are accessible globally in multiple formats. I believe she would be pleased.

I don't think that it's too late for you to change yourself, that your habits are too deeply rooted or that you're too old to experiment with odd and difficult exercises. Not so! I know that anyone can learn a new skill at any age. José Silva, my dear friend, taught his students, "The brain is like a muscle. It will shrivel up if you don't use it. If you keep using it to explore new ideas, it will grow stronger." He also advised that the best method to build a new self was through meditation, affirmations, and self-help tapes. One of my favorite affirmations, which I repeat daily, is

Every atom in my body thrills to life to keep me well.
Every molecule within me carries health from cell to cell.
Cells and organs in all systems built for lasting strength and youth.
Working in harmony together by the conscious light of truth.
from Thinking and Destiny by **Harold W. Percival**

When I taught Self-Awareness classes at my Center here in Alvarado, Texas, and while on the lecture circuit, I always stressed that everyone should question everything. "Accept nothing on faith— DISCERN! DISCERN! DISCERN!" I repeated.

I learned not to listen to negative thoughts. Energy is wasted on worrying about the expectation of unpleasant things, possible or impossible, on bad moods, unnecessary haste, nervousness, and irritability. I suggested the students say, "CANCEL! CANCEL!" if they thought or heard something negative. This idea is certainly not new, but I sincerely hope that you accept and practice it, for it's an excellent attitude adjustment.

When my serious search for self-awareness began, I was in my late forties. I was reading three books at a time to catch up on all the information and suggestions I had somehow missed or overlooked. Today I jot down all the meditations and affirmations that I feel will be of benefit for me. I make a list and read it every day until it becomes second nature for me. I'll share a few of the things I have on my list.

STOP the flow of aimless what-ifs, especially if they are negative thoughts.

COUNT my blessings. A good car, plenty of friends that I can share my sometimes offbeat concepts with, the weird sense of humor that makes me laugh out loud (or do I have a jester from a past life that continues to amuse me?).

OBSERVE and listen to others. Sometimes it's best not to say a word (and that's hard for me to do at times).

ADMIT I have faults, even if I think the song written by one of the best country western singers about being humble was composed with me in mind.

RELAX every muscle not in use at the moment. My favorite way to relax is off with the bra and no more pantyhose. I like wiggling my unrestricted toes with sheer joy.

MEALTIME preparation is a time to be creative. Always add spice to liven up the taste and boost up the body's energies.

LET everyone be. My biggest fall is thinking I know what's best for others. Look at it as *their* Learning Experience.

Over the past fifty years of reading books about metaphysics, psychology, and psychic abilities, I would like to share one particular book that made a profound impression on me. Elmer and Alice Green's *Beyond Biofeedback* has convinced me that, even without the machinery of feedback, I can benefit from the autogenic exercises.

When I read that Elmer and Alyce Green's research led them to believe that raising the temperature of one's hands has a beneficial effect on the body—that it can cure high blood pressure, steady the heart, and control headaches—I did a double-take. I've had a small heating pad beside my chair for years. Whenever I feel cold, I heat the pad and let the palms of my hands rest on it. It relaxes and spreads warmth through my entire body, giving me a cozy, comfortable feeling. I'd never heard or read that warming the hands could affect the entire body before reading it in their book. I did it intuitively, and I still do it today. I was pleased to read that the Green's research confirmed it.

I just thought of a poem I wrote on my 75th birthday. I guess it still applies today. I sent a copy of it to fifteen different magazines as filler. Six published the poem, and for the next three months, I received checks for $10 to $15, and from one, I actually got $20.

Where's Grandma?
In the dim and distant past
When the tempo wasn't fast
Grandma used to rock and knit
Crochet, read, and babysit
In those past days of gracious living
Grandma was the one for giving

When the family was in a jam
They could always count on 'gram'
Today you'll find her at the gym
Swimming, cycling to keep trim
Nothing these days seems to stop her
Now that Grandma's off her rocker!

Some days when I get up, I feel confident, perky, and so upbeat I'm tempted to walk to the mall and shop till I drop. I feel so cocky that I forget that I am old and wrinkled, that I must walk slowly, watch where I go because I might fall. I'm not foolhardy, just sensible.

Speaking of falling, some of my friends have suggested I use a cane, but I know, though I haven't said it out loud, that the reason I won't consider a cane is because I feel myself to be straight, tall, strong, and healthy, not a stooped old woman of eighty-two.

Sure, there are days that I have to con myself that it's the weather that's draining me of my energy. I have to mentally work overtime to get this body comfortable so I can get on and enjoy my daily living. When I have one of my 'off' days, and get in my recliner and talk to my body or listen to the healing tape or repeat and visualize the affirmation from Harold Percival.

You want to know what makes me **GLAD**? I discovered that being old and living alone has definite advantages because I can assure you, you're going to find them too when you get to be my age. How about going to bed and sleeping as long as you choose? Curling up with a good book and not having to fix a five-course dinner for the family. Doing things because you want to, not because you have to. Being in charge of the remote. Listening to classical music as loudly as you please. Talking on the phone as long as you want. If you have the need to socialize, go to the Senior Center in your area to play bridge, share a buffet, take a class in painting, writing, or Spanish.

Since I want to get this book written and I love being by myself, I'm getting more selective with whom I spend my time with. My favorite day of the week is still Wednesday when I go to Toastmasters. Every person in the group is like an extended family member

NOTE: Another thing Helene and I have in common. I have been a Toastmaster for fifteen years and have even volunteered as President. I highly recommend you find your local club and attend as a guest.

My son Chris comes every afternoon at 5:00 p.m. to play Canasta with me. That keeps my mind stimulated in sharp. I even occasionally let him win. I also have a stack of Word Puzzle books I like to fill out. Television is a last resort if I want to be entertained. It has to be a good program to hold my interest. I'd rather read a book.

Summing up some of my moods, the Glad, Mad, and Sad ones I shared with you today is just the start of my exciting life. I can't wait to find out what I am led to share with you tomorrow.

CONFESSIONS OF AN 83-YEAR-OLD SAGE

BE CAREFUL WHAT YOU PRAY FOR

I awoke at 9:00 a.m. this morning with the sun filtering through the semi-open blinds. As I looked toward the window, I could see the leaves gently swaying on the live oak and two squirrels playing 'Catch Me If You Can' on the limbs. There were no birds in sight. Guess they had an early breakfast. I slipped on my house shoes, the kind that have arch support, are open-toed and have a heel strap. The first thought that popped into my head was, "No more strapless inch-high scuffs for me." They were the cause of my fall in June last year when my high heel twisted, and I fractured my back. I spent three days in the hospital and a month at home recuperating with physical therapy. It was a hopeless, helpless feeling, flat on my back. There were times that I wished I could leave this body and go to a better place.

"Slow down. Your body is no longer spring chicken", I remember my mother always telling my dad. He was always in a hurry to get up and go, too.

OK mom, I got the message.

This morning the body is telling me to have a cup of green tea with a slug of pomegranate juice. Did you know that pomegranate juice is good for the system? It cleanses the gunk that sticks to the walls of the arteries. I slipped a slice of seven-grain bread into the toaster, got the applesauce out of the fridge, cut a piece of cheese, and carried my breakfast tray over to the chair by the window.

Where did my idea of what to eat this morning come from? I've learned to listen to what my body needs and to act accordingly. When I listen and observe, I always learn something. It's stimulating to be alert and aware. That is what I mean when I say, "*Learn to live, not just exist.*"

Are you ready for a lesson about ESP this morning? How many of you think that ESP means Extra Sensory Perception? Sorry about that. To me, it means Effective Sensory PERCEPTION and Extra Sensory PROJECTION. We all have the ability. It's just not developed through practice and recognized by everyone.

If you stay with me and you have the desire to learn more about what makes you *'tick, click and get sick,'* I will guide you through techniques and share with you a number of examples that may spark your interest. You may even wish to investigate.

Remember one of my favorite affirmations I shared with you earlier that tells the body how to stay healthy? What would you say if I told you that there is a book that is specific and alphabetically covers the emotional causes for physical illness and the metaphysical way to approach your specific problem? The title of the book is *Heal Your Body* by Louise Hay. The book is like an encyclopedia. It is formatted into three columns. The first is the *Problem* which lists every disease. The second is the emotional connection, the *Probable Cause*. The third is the affirmation to be repeated to create *New Thought Patterns*. An example is; if cancer is the <u>Problem</u> and the <u>Probable Cause</u> is deep hurt, longstanding resentment, a deep secret, or grief eating away at the self or carrying hatred. What's the use of carrying around all that negative baggage? The <u>New Thought Pattern</u> that one needs to repeat is "I lovingly forgive and release all of the past. I choose to fill my world with joy. I love and approve of myself."

When I share or suggest to people that they read the book *Heal Your Body* I find that most of them are in denial, and the Probable Cause, according to them, does not apply to their condition. So let me rephrase my statement.

"Have you ever considered what you're thinking may have caused your illness?"

Frank Outlaw summed it up so clearly with his insightful explanation:

Watch your thoughts, they become words.
Watch your words, they become actions.
Watch your actions, they become habits.
Watch your habits, they become character.
Watch your character, for it becomes your destiny.

I'm certainly not suggesting that you ignore the advice of your certified medical practitioner when you have a physical challenge. They serve a useful purpose, but for some reason, the word practitioner sets up a red flag and reminds me that they are practicing what they have been taught. We are uniquely different. Some of our symptoms may be triggered by emotion, by our environment, and the current scientific thinking is that our genes affect our physical manifestations. 'Physician Heal Thyself' *after* you assimilate everyone's opinion comes to mind. But that is my personal mindset.

And what about prayer, beseeching a higher power like God? Does it work? Definitely! Thoughts have energy. Words have energy. When we think or say something with emotion, it manifests more swiftly. Some emotions that are especially powerful include love, hate, fear, pain, and anger. I must also include MAD, SAD, or GLAD.

Are you familiar with a Novena? In the Catholic tradition, a Novena is a prayer to a saint, Jesus, or the Virgin Mary. You must attend mass and recite the rosary for nine days if you want or need something. You will get an answer or even a material object if that's what you petition for.

I was born and raised a Catholic, and as a child, I put Novenas to the test. I had so much luck and so many coincidences that happened; I got the reputation of being a witch or the luckiest kid on the block. I gave the Virgin Mary all the credit for answering my Novenas. In my book, *In Contact With Other Realms*, I go into more detail about how the Virgin Mary granted my wish for a sack of candy.

The following is a true story that made me have second thoughts of the Virgin Mary was responsible for one of my dear friend's husband getting the mumps

Elizabeth was very naive when I met her. She led a sheltered life in a devoutly Catholic family. After she married her childhood sweetheart, it didn't take long for her to become pregnant. Ten months after the birth of her first child, she had a second child, and ten months after that, a third. The third child was born with serious problems, heart, and brain damage, to name a couple of the challenges. Elizabeth developed extreme guilt. She thought it was her fault that the baby had so many physical problems, that it was because she enjoyed sex too much and that God was punishing her. This took place in the early 1950s when church dogma was against birth control, and so many people still took 'hook, line and thinker' whatever the church decreed. Elizabeth decided that she would no longer have sex with her husband. She spent all of her time taking care of the child and neglecting her family. She would not listen when the doctor explained that it was not her fault, that her body was depleted of vital minerals, and her being pregnant was a drain on her system. The child died at six months of age. Elizabeth now felt that her penance was complete. We were relieved that she was back to being normal whenever your idea of normal is. She began attending mass every morning.

One afternoon when we met in the park to watch her children play, she told me that she had made a Novena to the blessed mother that everything would be fine.

One of the stipulations of making an arena was that you were to tell no one about it until it manifested.

It was several weeks later when her husband, Charles, complained about his jaw hurting. The next morning he had the mumps. The following morning is groin was swollen. He was one miserable dude.

A week later, she told me that she made a Novena that Charles would get the mumps. She read someplace that when men get the mumps, they become sterile.

"Elizabeth, tell me you didn't actually make such a Novena. The mumps could have damaged the brain. It really could have been serious," I explained.

I will swear on a stack of Saint James bibles that this was her reply. "I wasn't the one who gave Charles the mumps; the Blessed Mother did."

"Don't tell anyone, especially don't tell Charles," I advised her. "Let it be our secret."

We never mentioned it again.

A number of years later, Charles came home and announced that he had a physical by the company doctor. When the doctor heard that he'd had the mumps as an adult, he told them there was now a procedure by which they can inject live sperm in the testicles and that Charles would be capable of fathering a child.

It was time to tell Charles what the Blessed Mother did. I cracked up when she told me the exact words he had to say to her.

"Elizabeth, I'm glad that you waited to tell me this because I would have killed you had you told me when I went through the agony of the mumps."

Question: Who is responsible for Charles getting the mumps?

Was it the Blessed Mother? Or was it the intense desire that Elizabeth projected mentally and emotionally?

Are you using your ESP in a positive way? If not, better give it a second thought.

I hope this makes you realize just how powerful your thoughts actually are.

Confession of an 83-Year-Old Sage

I'M NOT A DOCTOR, BUT...

This morning I decided to watch the local news as I'm having a bowl of cottage cheese and cantaloupe with my decaf for breakfast.

The weatherman predicted a long hot summer, but that's not unusual in Texas. With the air conditioner, fans, and iced tea, I will survive.

"Let me be a channel to help people help themselves," was the affirmation I said aloud as I sat by the window.

A funny thing happens when I repeat that phrase. Sometimes it is an unexpected person at my door. Other times, it's a letter that needs to be answered. This morning it was a phone call from a former student that attended one of my workshops when I was in Michigan on the lecture circuit years ago.

"I met you twenty-four years ago," she said. "I don't expect you to remember me, but I just ran across your book, *The Name It & Claim It Game*, that I've read and reread. That's what prompted me to call you. I know you can help me."

"I'm 76-years-old, and for the past several months, my legs feel like rubber, my mind is fuzzy, and it's an effort to get out of bed in the morning."

The first impression I got while I was listening to her was that her body is toxic. I never diagnose anyone because I feel so strongly that one should be able to get their own answers.

"Have you seen a doctor?" I asked.

"Yes, I had a complete physical a month ago. The doctor told me there was nothing wrong with me, and I just needed to slow down and get a hobby to keep my mind occupied."

"Do you own a foot massager? You know the type that you fill with warm water, and that vibrates the bottom of your feet."

"I know the kind you're talking about. I've seen them in the drugstore, but I don't own one," she replied.

"Have you considered that perhaps your body is toxic and that it is in need of cleansing to help release the toxins?" I inquired.

There was a brief pause before she continued. "Mrs. Hadsell, you're the second person that told me that my body might be toxic. In fact, a member of the Red Hat Society, of which I am a member, gave me some pads that she said are used by the Chinese to remove toxins. Have you ever heard about that? Do you think that would help?"

"I'm not familiar with the pads, but I do know that there's a detox tea on the market that is sold in health food stores. You have a lot of choices to help heal the body. If you do choose to use the foot massager, I suggest that you add one-fourth cup of Epsom salts to the water and vibrate your feet for 15 minutes, twice a day, for a couple of days, and then you can do it once a day before bedtime. I hope whatever you choose to do helps."

End of our conversation. How interesting that she had her friend also suggests that she may be toxic. Was that a coincidence?

GET THE SWATTER

I woke up this morning feeling hungry. I don't know what triggered it, but 'eat healthy' turned into 'eat hearty.' I fixed two scrambled eggs, a slice of seven-grain bread with orange marmalade, and tea.

The wildlife sanctuary outside my window is quiet and still, not a critter insight and no breeze. It's a good day to enjoy the air conditioner and finish reading my book.

As I find myself still thinking about the woman who'd called and the coincidence (or not) of her friend's mentioning the possibility that she was toxic, I became aware of her fly that was vying for my attention. In fact, it was so bold it was circling around the rim of the tea mug that I was holding my hand.

I shooed the pest away. All of a sudden, my brain seemed to be taking pictures, as if it were a camera clicking scenes that occurred in the past and waiting for my feelings to catch up. I started to grin as I let the memories surface.

I was six years old, sitting in church with my dad, when I saw fly on the fat neck of the man who sat in front of us. I put it there, and he was trying to slap it away.

I snickered, and my dad bent down and asked me what was wrong.

I whispered, "The fly on the man's neck."

People around us began to stare as the priest was giving the Sunday sermon, and we were creating a distraction. Then I got *the look*; you know the look that someone gives you that means Be Quiet. I folded my hands in my lap and bowed my head until, at long last, I heard 'Amen,' and people were getting up to leave.

"Young lady, what was that all about?" My dad questioned as we walked home from church.

"I put a fly on the fat man's neck," I proudly announced.

"This is the middle of winter, and there are no flies," my dad explained.

"Not a real fly—a pretend fly. Uncle Andrew told me I could do it, and when I did it, the man would try to slap it away, and he did."

"That's nonsense. Your uncle was joking."

"But I saw it. Honest, I did."

"Well, if you thought you saw it, you were mistaken. In the future, try to listen to the priest. That's why we go to church."

That afternoon I went across the alley to where my grandparents lived, and Uncle Andrew, who was then 16-years-old, was putting air into his bicycle tires.

"Uncle Andrew, I saw fly on the neck of the man that sat in front me at church this morning. Dad doesn't believe me. Is that a play-like game?"

"I guess it is. I do it for the fun of it when I get bored. In school, I can pull the pigtails of the girls that sit in front of me. I know that they can feel it 'cause they look around to see who's pulling their hair. Just don't tell anyone if you do it next time. They won't understand."

I didn't tell anyone, but there were occasions when I tried it again, and it worked.

But what about a physical fly? What should I do? I tried communicating with them, and they just seemed to ignore me. I realize that their lifespan is 30 days if they're lucky, but if they continue to be a pest after several warnings, I am forced to take drastic measures.

I've rationalized that they are here for learning experiences, as we all are, and the only way they will learn to quit pestering people is to keep their distance or suffer the consequences.

I got up to get the fly swatter.

ENCOUNTER WITH A FELLOW TRAVELER

It was 7:05 a.m. when I awoke this morning. I felt that it was urgent that I explain more about mental telepathy, projection, and concentration.

I'll back up and review the mental picture of the fly I projected onto the neck of the man in the church when I was 6-years-old. I saw the fly and pretended that it was crawling around. The man picked up my thought and could feel the fly. Not really such a big deal. What I found to be a BIG! BIG! deal was being able to visualize and project an object and another person thinking it to be in the physical.

The following is one of my fun projects. You may want to try it sometime to find out how strong your power of concentration is.

It was 1966. I was on a lecture tour. During the day, I had free time, so the malls, parks, and art galleries were where I chose to spend my time. My favorite mental game during my travels at that time was to develop my power of concentration.

To start out, I sat quietly and studied my hand with such intensity that I became oblivious of not only my surroundings but also noises and smells. It took a lot of practice, but I was thrilled to finally be able to do it. One thing I hadn't expected was to 'become one' with my hand and actually see through it. I could see the blood moving through my veins as if I had a bird's eye view of the branches of a river. The bones of all sizes were locked together yet able to move freely. It was awesome!

The next technique was to imagine an object, mentally place it on the table or floor, and concentrate on it until it became so real that someone else could see it. This is called illusion. The person doing the projection becomes so adept they can influence everyone in their immediate area to see what they project. Fakirs in India are masters of illusion. My goal, however, was to be able to hold an object in one spot with concentration and make it appear so solid one would think it was the real thing and attempt to pick it up.

I confess I had made a number of attempts at this experiment without success, but this day was different

I was in Boston at a park two blocks from my hotel, ready to experiment with a newly acquired talent. I sat on a bench and mentally projected a $5 gold piece on the sidewalk. I used that object because it was something that would draw attention to a passerby and make them want to bend down to pick it up.

Feeling confident that I had projected enough energy to make the gold piece look real, I began to study the people that walked past. I noticed a young mother and her son coming. Evidently, the child, who must have been about three years of age, was tired of being in his stroller. He was holding on to the side while his mother guided it.

They walked at a slow pace. All of a sudden, the child's face lit up, and he stopped to reach down for my gold piece. He kept trying to retrieve it, but nothing happened. The mother looked down to investigate what he was trying to pick up.

"Honey, there is nothing there," she said.

He made several more attempts without success. All of a sudden, he looked up at me and gave me the biggest grin as if he knew I had something to do with his behavior. I was elated as I realized I had been successful.

"If just one more person could confirm for me that my experiment worked," I thought.

I didn't have a long wait. An elderly man leisurely strolled my way, perhaps out for his daily walk. He appeared to be deep in thought and oblivious to all other people passing. Suddenly he paused, for what seemed to be half a second, and looked down on the sidewalk ahead of him. His eyes opened wide as he paused to take a second look at my projected gold piece.

But he didn't stoop to pick it up instead; he turned, grinned at me, and said, "Young lady, I know what you were doing, but you can't fool a Fellow Traveler."

This is a fun experiment if you are interested in developing concentration. Again I remind you to practice, practice, practice.

While I was in Russia, I learned from the professor who was conducting experiments with volunteers that one out of every forty-three people could accomplish this feat within five minutes. The rest of the groups, with practice, were all able to do it within a three-month period.

POINTS TO PONDER

This morning I awoke in a reflective mood. It is 10:30 a.m. The sky is overcast. Last evening I received a phone call from someone out of the past—twenty years to be exact. A former neighbor called to tell me she was in town.

"I'm here to pay old debts, and you're one of the people I still owe," she said.

After fixing my decaf and grabbing a banana, I headed for my window chair. As I looked out to see if there was any action in the bird or squirrel world, it began to rain. The rain hit the windows and taps and spatters, small and countable, and then it was everywhere, banging on the metal roof and filling the downspouts. As I sat and listened, I began vividly recalling and reliving the time when I first met Laura.

It was by the rural mailboxes across the road from where we lived. She told me they had bought the old Hunter house next to my property.

"We are his, hers, and ours family of eight," she explained. Don has two by his first wife, I have three by my ex, and the youngest, Glenn, who is six, is our offspring."

I invited her to come have coffee with me the next morning so we could get better acquainted.

She accepted. "I won't bring the 'troops.'" That was the word she used when referring to the children.

It's funny how much I can remember about her after that first meeting. It seems like yesterday she sat in the granny rocker facing me. She was 34-years-old, a big woman, structured to the Amazonian scale, the kind Dior and fashion magazines turned their backs on in utter horror. Her hair, mouse gray, lacked body and hung helter-skelter to her shoulders. The face could not be called beautiful, but it was striking, with prominent cheekbones and a wide jaw, which triangulated into a weak chin. Her lips were thin and the

41

eyes searching, with anticipation, for answers—why am I here, and is this all there is?

I've heard the question hundreds of times over the years from my students.

She told me she grew up on a farm in Oklahoma with three brothers and one sister. She was the oldest and had the responsibilities of cooking, washing, and seeing that her brothers and baby sister got to school on time. Her dad drank, and her mother was in bed most of the time with headaches and dizzy spells.

"I got out of there as soon as I could. I married at seventeen, right after I graduated. My ex worked for an oil company, and we moved every three or four months. It was exciting at first, but when the drinking started, I split."

She was eager to have someone to listen to her story. "Do you have any chocolate candy? It's my fix when things get too hectic," she said, giggling like a child.

"I just happened to have a bag of Hershey's Kisses," I replied and got up to get it. She already had two cups of coffee and a piece of carrot cake, which she devoured in twenty seconds, but she took the sack when I handed it to her.

She was giving me the opportunity to be a 'do-gooder,' and I accepted the part. We talked about religion, prayer, and church. All of a sudden, she reared back in the rocker and gave me her opinion about God. It was her description that one could not easily forget. It went something like this.

"God likes torturing people. He does it in a sneaky way by sending you a Guardian Angel, or two, or three, to mess with your head. So what is right or wrong is never cut and dried."

She never seemed to know what to do with her hands. Her voice was strangled, abrupt, and often hard to hear. As I sat and studied her, she reminded me of a whipped puppy, and my heart went out to her as I tried to find the right words that she could relate to.

Ten minutes after she left, I sat at the kitchen table, staring down at what was left of the candy sack. She had eaten about ten or twelve pieces, but who's counting? On her way out, I told her to take the bag. She said I should keep it in case she got stranded without a car, and she could count me satisfying fix.

Behind me, the fridge was humming in the instant hot water maker stopped boiling and snapped off. I remember telling myself it's because I'm in the mood for a cup of chamomile tea to calm me down, but my subconscious didn't buy it for a second. A recurring question ricocheted around my brain—how could I help her?

School was out for the summer, and the 'troops' were over here at my place most of the day. I didn't mind because I didn't have any grandchildren that lived nearby. We read, played games, and the two older girls helped me with light housekeeping, which I paid them for. It was a fun experience for all of us.

I never met Laura's husband. The children told me that the dad worked in town and had a second job as a night guard at one of the industrial complexes.

It was after school started when Laura started to come over to visit again. I shared some of my research and concepts in the field of self-awareness. She only half listened, and I got the impression she was more interested in my Hershey stash. I remember giving her the book *The Power of Positive Thinking* by Norman Vincent Peale and encouraging her to read it.

"I'd really like your opinion on what he has to say. We can discuss it," I suggested.

We never got to review it.

The last contact I had with Laura was when she called one morning. She spoke in a broken whisper and said that she wanted to see me.

My first thought was that she was out of candy.

For several days I've been gathering my thoughts and writing them down. I titled the piece *Points to Ponder*. I intended to pass out copies to students at an awareness class I was invited to teach. I'd even gone to Office Depot to get special paper with a colored rainbow background to print the copies on.

When Laura came over that day, she told me that she had a job; her husband lost his daytime job, and they were in a financial bind. She was in a hurry to leave. We hugged as I handed her a sack of miniature Hershey bars.

"Hey, wait a minute," I said. "I'd like to give you a copy of something I wrote for my class."

I handed it to her as she walked out the door.

"Thanks." She smiled, putting up her best defense. Not an annoyed smile, a jaded smile, or even an angry get-outta-my-face-you-busybody smile, just a nice, courteous smile.

It was three days later when her oldest daughter came over to tell me that her mother was gone and that they were moving. She, her sister, and her brother were going to live with a grandmother.

"Nobody knows where mother went." were her parting words as she turned to leave.

And now, twenty years later, I would hear what happened to her. She and her children were my thoughts over the years, but I never pursued it.

When she arrived promptly at one, I was momentarily speechless. I didn't recognize her. Forty pounds lighter, a new hairstyle, and a genuine smile, she handed me a gift-wrapped box.

"It's a present," she grinned. When I opened it, there was a crystal-covered dish full of Hershey's Kisses.

She told me about her mental breakdown and that she lived in Colorado, Arizona, and Nevada. It was all a blur until she met someone who encouraged her to seek help for her mood swings.

"I now realize you were trying to help me understand what life on this planet is all about, but I wasn't ready," she admitted.

She reached into her purse and handed me a folded piece of paper. It was yellowed with age.

I must have looked bewildered.

"Open it, open it," she encouraged.

As I cautiously spread it open, I recognized the faded rainbow background on the paper and the *Points to Ponder* thoughts I had written twenty years earlier.

"You kept this all these years?" I was dumbfounded.

"I couldn't throw it away. Occasionally I'd read it. The more I read it, the more sense it made for me. I now understand and appreciate all you did for me and the children."

"And how are the 'troops'?" I blurted out.

She began telling me what each one was doing, that she had three grandchildren, and the girls often spoke about the summer they spent by the lake.

And what are the *Points to Ponder* that answered the questions for Laura? The following is a copy of what I still pass out to students when I teach self-awareness classes.

Points to Ponder

- When we choose to be born (most souls choose their parents), we receive a body. You may like it or hate it, but it will be yours for as long as you live in this dimension. How you take care of it, or fail to take care of it, can make an enormous difference in the quality of her life.

- You will learn many lessons, for you have enrolled in a full-time informal school called LIFE IN THE PHYSICAL. Each day you will be presented with opportunities to learn what you need to know. The lessons presented are often completely different from those you THINK you need.

- There are no mistakes—only lessons. Growth is a process of trial and error. You may learn as much from failure as you can from success. Maybe more. You can choose to learn easily with joy and acceptance or learn the hard way, pain and resistance. Trust that everything happens for a reason.

- A lesson is repeated until it is learned. Do you ever get the feeling that the faces or places are different, but the situation and feelings you have about them are the same? For

45

instance, have you changed jobs frequently because there was always a person there who just rubbed you the wrong way? When you realize that it is this opportunity to learn and move beyond this recurring problem, you can choose the right solution, thereby 'passing the test,' so to speak. And you know that running from them doesn't solve problems. It is then that you have learned your lesson. When you have learned it (as evidenced by the change in your attitude and ultimately your behavior), then you can go on to the next lesson. LEARNING lessons does not end. As long as you live, there will be something more to learn.

- 'THERE' is no better than 'HERE.' You will simply discover another 'THERE' that will again look better to you than your 'HERE.' Don't be fooled into believing that the unattainable is better than what you already have. You can choose to always be present in the HERE and in the THERE. Gratefulness and acceptance do wonders for your state of mind and will help you move past unwanted situations.

- Others are merely mirrors of you. You cannot love or hate anything about another person unless it reflects something you love or hate about yourself. When tempted to judge or criticize others, look inside yourself for the exact quality and meditate on that. We are all here as both teachers and students to help each other learn, so take the opportunity when it comes your way.

- What you make of your life is up to you. You have all the tools and resources you need.

- What you create with those tools and resources is up to you. This may sound trite, but it is true. Through the universal law of attraction, you attract to yourself what you focus on.

- Look at life as one learning experience after another.

DOWN MEMORY LANE

I'd better apologize up front because today I'm going down memory lane, and I guess it's not a really bad thing to do except… you won't be able to share with me some of the memories you recall with your children while they were growing up. And I truly would like to hear them.

What triggers this mood? I guess it was the cantaloupe and cottage cheese with half an English muffin I'm having with green tea for breakfast this morning.

When my son, Dike, was two years old, he loved cantaloupe. In fact, he was the only one of my three children that acquired the taste and preferred it over my chocolate chip cookies. He called it 'lope.' He couldn't pronounce the word cantaloupe. Yes, he can pronounce it today. The kid is a 58-year-old man now.

As I sit and eat each piece, I began recalling some incidents that still stick in my memory bank about the children as they were growing up.

The Day Chris Saw God

How can I ever forget the day my son Chris, three and a half years old, saw God.

It was Good Friday—a MAJOR EVENT in the Catholic Church. Dike was in the second grade, and Pam, the oldest, was in the fourth grade at the Catholic school. I had promised Chris that I would take him to church for the first time. "But you have to sit and be quiet," I explained.

Before the service began, the ritual was for the Monsignor to walk down the aisle and sprinkle holy water while the servers (two altar boys) waved around gold balls filled with incense back and forth, following the Monsignor.

The Monsignor, who was huge—well over six feet and almost three hundred pounds—wore a purple cape trimmed in gold with a foot-tall

47

head cap. As he passed our pew (we sat on an aisle seat), the sprinkled water landed on Chris' face.

Chris sat with his mouth open as he took in the unfamiliar surroundings. The Monsignor mumbled in Latin as he passed. The choir was chanting in Latin in the loft—all so foreign to him.

After the walk around the church aisles was completed, the Monsignor went to the vestibule to change. He came out to begin the mass in his regular robes. That's when Chris looked up at me and asked, "Where did God go?"

That's all he talked about for the rest of the day. When my husband, Pat, got home that evening, Chris climbed into his lap to chatter.

"God used a sprinkler on me today," he said.

Dike was standing nearby and voiced his opinion. "That wasn't God. It was Father Bernard."

Pam had to chime in too. "Once, when I sat in the front row, I got sprinkled too."

"You did not see God," Dike repeated.

"Well, where is he then?" Chris asked.

"God is in heaven," Pam said.

"But mama told me that heaven is right here."

Pat just listened and grinned.

It Was The Right Thing To Do

Dike and his friend, Michael (both 12 years old), were playing catch in the street in front of our house. It was a dead-end street, and there was very little traffic. All of a sudden, I heard a crash and ran to investigate. The ball broke the neighbor's picture window. The neighbor came out yelling and demanded to know who did it. Now all the neighbors were out to watch.

"I did it," Dike said.

"Well, you're going to pay for it," the irate neighbor shouted. (Guess the noise of the shattered glass woke him up from his nap.)

Pat said he would take care of it.

When we got back into the house, Pat reminded Dike he was told not to play on the street, to play in the school ground, which was only a block away. After giving him a sermon about responsibility, honesty, obligation, etc., Pat told him his weekly allowance of $1 would be cut to $0.50 a week until the window was paid for.

"Dad, I didn't throw the ball. Michael got mad, and he broke the window."

"Then why didn't you say so?"

"Because Michael's dad would beat him with his leather belt, and he asked me to say I did it."

"How do you know that Michael's dad beats him?"

"I'm in the gym with Michael, and I've seen the black and purple welts on his back and legs. He tells the kids that he fell over his brother's wagon."

"I'll look into it," my husband said. And he did in his own way. My husband was one of those concerned citizens who, when he was aware of an injustice, he did something about it. No, he didn't carry a gun—he notified the proper authorities until the problem was resolved.

This happened in the late fifties. There was no law about disciplining our children at the time. Thank God that law has changed today.

Pam's First Boy Crush

She was fifteen at the time. A pimple-faced lanky kid had a crush on her. He threw the morning paper from his bicycle every morning before school started. He would pass our house at about 6:00 a.m. I noticed Pam was up every morning at 6:00 a.m., sitting on the deacon's bench on the front porch. Some mornings it was so cold she wrapped herself in a blanket. When I asked her why she was up so early, she replied, "I like the fresh morning air."

Later I discovered she had her closet floor stacked with unopened papers. Oh yes, she had tied them with a pink ribbon. Isn't first love groovy?

Do you call the incident I wrote about the neighbor lady and her fix on chocolate? Well, I, too, needed a fix when the afternoon 'daze' began. I would have a cup of chamomile tea and suck on a Tootsie Roll Pop. Now isn't that better than smoking, drinking, or taking pills to cope?

My husband and the kids were aware of my tea and sucker quick fix. One day I really had a trying day, and Pam seemed to be the target, or she thought she was. She sat on the front porch on the deacon's bench in pouted.

When my husband got home that evening, I overheard a complaint as he walked in the door. "Be prepared, dad; this has been one of mom's three sucker days."

So what was or still might be your fix? You don't have to answer that. This is my confession, and I'm letting it all out. So you're not interested? Then why in tarnation are you reading this? The cover alerted you that it was a confession book.

There I go again with another one of my compulsive disorders, thinking that I know what you're thinking. I'm right, aren't I?

FADED BEAUTY

Last night I set the alarm to get up at 8:00 a.m. My granddaughter and her two children were coming to spend the day. I always look forward to their visits, but I had an unusually restless night, and this morning I felt exhausted.

I headed for the shower. Maybe this would put the starch back into me, I rationalized. I needed all the help I could conjure up to face the day.

Well, it helped. After I dried myself off, I said at the dressing table to put on some fake-up.

As I looked into the mirror to see myself—I mean really see myself—my eyes stared back at my reflection. What used to be beautiful is now old, tired and withered. Dark circles line dull brown eyes, stringy salt and pepper hair hangs limp against my face; my skin is pallid and flaky despite pampering myself with Cindy Crawford beauty products. Then I noticed something, the years it hollowed my cheeks a little, but no passage of time or conflict with grief could have altered my firm mouth and determined chin. When it registered, I smiled so wide it hurt my face.

I began thinking about my granddad, how I loved to go visit him on the farm when I was a child. He had so many interesting stories to tell—how he came to American from Germany to grow wheat; how fortunate I was to be born in America.

In his declining years, he spoke in non-sequiturs. It was better to play along. I must have been about 9-years-old. I recall thinking the elderly are spooky when they degenerate into reflections of their younger selves. They say things that make sense on some grammatical level but are not always connected to reality.

His skin was stained and wrinkled, but his blue eyes were strikingly clear. Some gray hair gathered above each year in his posture was an ongoing conversation with gravity.

He wasn't old. He was ancient.

I wondered how I registered with my two great-granddaughters.

After they arrived, I observed and studied their behavior. They reminded me of a chameleon, constantly changing their colors, and I never knew which shade was coming next.

"I'm hungry."

"I'm bored."

"I want to play checkers."

"I want to go outside."

"I want to color."

"I want to play ping pong."

"I am hungry."

"I want to go home."

Precious girls bubbling with enthusiasm. I was pleased and proud at how intelligent, well-mannered, and mature they were for their ages of eleven and seven. Their parents are doing an excellent job. During their eight-hour stay, I ventured to guess my granddaughter, and I had a max of an hour and a half without interruption, but that's the beauty of being a caring woman and mother.

Before I close this insightful sharing with you on yesterday in yesteryear, I'd like to leave this thought:

I discovered an advantage of growing old. I've been there, done that, and it was a beautiful learning experience. Now, I just want to sit down with my feet up and let my granddaughter make and bring me a cup of green ginseng tea.

I can watch the children set the table while their mother cut up a watermelon and opens a container of pasta and sandwiches for lunch.

I can close my eyes and get a quickie five-minute nap to regroup before anyone notices.

See how much you have looked to look forward to when you reach my age?

DANCING ON THE EDGE

Some days I feel like a nut, not the run-of-the-mill plain goober, but a macadamia, a cut above the rest of the nut family.

I just want a V8 and a hard-boiled egg to get a jump start on my day. So this is what my breakfast was this morning.

Remember that this book is about confessing some of my inner thoughts and actions. Well, it's time to reveal another one on my compulsive disorders—I dance in the nude. And what I am saying is, I bare it all. The 82-year-old boobs that flip flop from breast to belly button, the round belly that rolls up and down, back and forward as a kick up my feet and twist my hips to the music in the lyrics of Freddy Fender. Michael Jackson could learn something by observing my gyrations.

It all started back in 1963 when I read Laura Huxley's book, *You Are Not The Target*. As I read all the benefits one could accomplish by dirty dancing, I did a visual in my mind and said, "Why not?"

I can just hear my two grown sons remark today when they find out what I've done behind closed doors all these years.

"Mother, that's gross!" or "Act your age!" Why is it that our children picture and expect us to be like the Ozzie and Harriet family, the TV sitcom depicting a goody-two-shoes family? Perhaps there are families that are prim, proper, and precise. That's not me. Today I have three philosophes

1. Life goes on.
2. Who cares? and…
3. Get real.

OOPS! There may be some repercussions from my sons because I'm certain they didn't have the foggiest notion that I've been a professional dancer for over forty years. They may change their names, disown me, or go into hiding. But I'll say it again, "Life goes on. Who cares? Get real."

Let's get back on track and explain why nude dancing is so beneficial.

When I take off my clothes, which these days are only a bra, half slip, dress or robe, and sensible shoes, I feel and pretend that I'm discarding all the ideas, feelings, compulsions, embarrassments, fears, and shame that have been superimposed upon me.

Through the naked dance, I expel all the unwanted, painful feelings that crop up from time to time. It's not a technique that will balance and solve all your hang-ups once and for all. It's an ongoing cleansing that I've learned to enjoy doing. Sometimes it's months before I dance. I seem to know when my body wants to release a buildup of thoughts and emotions that set up a 'pity party' feeling. A lot of time, I find it beneficial to drink a cup of chamomile tea and munch on a Hershey bar. But for the benefit of feeling more alive, feeling more in control, and more comfortable, it's nude dancing for me.

I must share the following true story that took place a number of years ago when one of the gals that attended my self-awareness workshop while I was on the lecture circuit.

She called asking if she could come to my Center to regroup. She was crying as she told me about a crisis she was going through. Her father died three weeks before, and a week later, her only brother died in an automobile accident.

"I can't sleep or eat. I stay so keyed up," she explained. "Can you help me?"

She lived in Oklahoma at the time, and it would be a five-hour drive to get here. When I told her that she was welcome, she got in her car and was at my doorstep shortly after dark on the same day.

"I don't want to eat anything," she said when I asked if she was hungry. I suggested that she sit on the couch, and we could talk. I knew she was expecting some words of wisdom that would solve her physical and mental dilemma. But I knew it would take more than words to release all her bottled-up emotions.

I knew what it would take… You guessed it; nude dancing.

Before she arrived, I got out my pad of paper and began writing the script; I would be the producer, director, and participant for her dancing role. Prompting and performing with her.

"Can you trust me and follow my instructions? I need your permission for what you were about to undertake."

For a moment, she studied me, probably wondering, "What is this all about?"

"I'll participate with you," I added.

"I'm going to put on a Freddy Fender CD, and we're going to dance to the music until we drop all the pent-up, unresolved issues that are presently hindering your well-being."

When I'm in my mode of counseling, it seems like I shift gears, and I can read every thought of the person I'm trying to help.

"Just follow and listen to my instructions as we take off all our clothes."

I pulled off my dress, and she followed suit.

I began, "You are the center of the world, and you will now recognize it. You were afraid, but now you will release it as you dance."

She took off her clothes and listened. I turned on the CD, low it first and we began dancing.

I began my prompting with the following key phrases:

"I am expelling fear!"

"I am expelling loneliness!"

"I am expelling injustice!"

"I am expelling uncertainty!"

"I am expelling the inability to express myself!

"I want to love: I want to be loved. I want to love: I want to be loved!"

After I repeated the above suggestions, I turned up the CD loud and suggested if she was led to shout out any bottled-up feelings or emotions to do so. We danced, shouted, laughed, and got hysterical until we both collapsed, out of breath.

"Now go to bed. You can shower in the morning, and we will discuss your healing. She slept for eighteen hours. I checked in on her several times, and she was sleeping like a baby.

Today I still hear from her. She still reminds me that I give her the fastest and most fun attitude adjustment she's ever had. She, too, still unwinds and stays centered by dancing nude. Don't knock it until you try it.

The answer is no—I have never tried this therapy on my male students.

I have another SINGLE SESSION THERAPY that has come to mind. It is a cartoon that got my attention. Although I have never tried it, at times, I've been tempted to give it my best shot.

The scene is a psychiatrist's office. A woman is sitting in an overstuffed chair, and the doctor is giving her a powerful slap on her face as he shouts, "Snap out of it!"

Do you have a senior friend that is subject to fatigue and illness and cannot ward off infections? The problem might be an immune deficiency. The immune system protects the body from bacteria, viruses, fungi, and other harmful organisms. Toxins in foods and the environment, poor diet, and unmanageable stress can all contribute to a decline in immune system activity. Strengthening your thymus gland is beneficial, which is located in the upper part of the chest behind the breastbone. The thymus is a nursery for immune system cells that can help fight infection. Unfortunately, this organ shrinks in size as we grow older, and its effectiveness gradually diminishes.

Here's a quick and easy exercise to stimulate your thymus gland to boost your immune system health. Every morning, tap the middle of your breastbone with your fingers for five minutes. I make it my daily ritual by keeping a three-minute egg timer by my chair. If I'm watching TV, I flip over the timer and watch the pink sand funnel into the bottom glass tube. I do it twice, three minutes each time. I know my body appreciates the extra effort I give it. Simple little things mean a lot as you grow older.

JUST WHO WAS JOAN OF ARC?

EVERYTHING IS POSSIBLE

Now, why would Shirley MacLaine come to mind this morning? Perhaps it's because I'm ready to go out on a limb and share an 'off the wall' experience. So, Shirley, move over; I, too, am a Cosmic Rover (one who has out-of-body experiences).

I'm having an oatmeal pancake with my decaf this morning. Ever tried adding an egg to leftover oatmeal, mixing it up, and frying it in olive oil greased pan? Add a few tablespoons of syrup, or I like to sprinkle it with a cinnamon and sugar mix. You'll never find that recipe at the International Pancake House; it's my granddaughter's.

Have you ever heard the expression, 'living in two different worlds?' I'd venture to guess that many of you have had that experience but chose not to discuss it, or you chalked it up as a fluke and forgot it.

David Letterman, Jay Leno, and Craig Ferguson, talk show hosts, are quick to dismiss the subject with humor whenever one of their guests brings up the subject that Shirley MacLaine so freely discusses. When I discuss 'far out' subjects, one of which I will share with you in a moment, and I see the raised eyebrows in the audience, I dismiss it by referring to my philosophy: *Life goes on. Who cares? Get over it.*

There are several other comments along that line that sum up a closed mind:

1. Loosen up your mindsets.
2. Get real. and
3. Get out of La La land.

How would you respond if I told you that ALL, not just a few science fiction stories and movies, are slowly introducing you to the future of this planet? That ought to scare the 'yell' out of a lot of people. I know it frightened me shoutless the first time I had an encounter of the lizard kind. Was it a thought form, an apparition? Tune in later, and I will share a true story of what happened with one of my friends who had an encounter with a lizard being from another planet.

Sorry about my digressing momentarily. I'll get on with what I want to share with you this morning.

"That's not her," I cried out in indignation when I saw the portrait of Joan of Arc displayed on the floor at a Sidewalk Art Show.

"Whoever painted this picture is completely off. Joan's nose was not that long... and look at the eyes... so cold."

My friend Ann, who accompanied me that day, just stood and looked at me for a moment and then asked, "Are you joking or serious? What brought that on?"

"Well, I guess I should know how she really looked," I softly replied as I stood for a moment trying to figure out where I was and what made me blurt out such a statement.

Evidently, I created a scene as several people moved in closer to see what was going on.

Back into the NOW... at the art exhibit... not in a scene where Joan and I were childhood friends. I was ready to move on.

"Just making a joke to lighten up, my friend," I sheepishly explained to everyone who heard my outburst.

The artist, a short chubby woman wearing a paint-stained smock, came over to me and handed me the wet brush she was using to paint the still life. "If you can capture the essence of her—of Joan of Arc, you are welcome to try."

"I'm not an artist, and I'm truly sorry if I caused you any embarrassment. Your work is unique," I stammered.

For a moment, she frowned. Then she began explaining. "This painting has been difficult for me since I first began it. I had a request from an elderly man to paint a portrait of Joan of Arc for him. I found it very challenging. I did this from some of the pictures I'd seen of her. The client did not like the painting. I've reworked it several times until I realized there would be no pleasing him. This was several years ago. Since that time, I've sold this painting three different times, and each time the buyer has brought it back. All of the buyer's explanations are the same. It doesn't fit with their decor, or the colors are wrong. I keep making changes, but evidently, I'm not able to capture something." She began cleaning the brush she was holding and placed it on the table.

"I'm sorry if I got so defensive a moment ago. Perhaps 'frustrated' would be a better way of explaining my feelings," she again apologized.

As my friend and I turned to leave her booth to grab my arm and said, "I want you to have his painting. Perhaps you can breathe life into her expression."

"No. No. I can't accept it. Someone may come in and relate to it," I answered, trying to refrain from gasping with surprise.

"If I don't sell the painting by the end of the month, I want you to have it as a gift." She took my telephone number and told me she would be in touch.

I dismissed the incident until I heard from her several weeks later.

"Come get your painting." She refused to take the money I offered.

After I took the painting home, I sat and began to study it. Suddenly, something happened, almost like the canvas came to life come in the faces with different features began appearing. I was witnessing a transfiguration on the canvas. In the past, it had been common for me to see changes of facial features in people, especially when someone is lecturing, but on a canvas, it was a little unusual. I could not relate to anyone that resembled Joan, the Joan I knew long ago. I set the canvas aside, waiting for inspiration. Nothing came.

I never hung the painting. Promising myself that I would get to it later, I sat on the floor against the wall in my office.

Several months later, I'm an artist, and I showed her the canvas.

"Perhaps you can do something with this painting," I suggested. She said she would take it and work on it. Three weeks later, the picture was returned.

"There is a message attached to this painting, and you are the only one it's meant for. Sorry I can't help you."

Now, my curiosity was aroused, and I had to pursue it further. I kept waiting for someone to appear that would rework the painting. That's when I got the idea to take it to a local art class. I told the teacher the students had my permission to, and anything with their creative imagination dictated. When I picked it up a week later, the background was painted blue instead of dark green. The color of Joan's blouse had been changed from rust to red, and the features were softer, but still, in my truth center, I knew it was not Joan.

I never felt inclined to hang it, so I stored 'Joan' in the garage. When we moved, I gave it to another consideration and took it with me for future study. Our next move was to our five-acre country home. It has remained there in the storage shed.

It's been forty years that the painting portrait has been in my possession. I haven't been in the shed for years, and I have given it no further thought... that is, until last year when I awoke after a vivid dream.

Three girls were playing tag; somehow, I felt I was one of them. When we all were exhausted, we sat down to rest and catch our breath. One girl looked at me and smiled, "I'm Joan. You are right that the picture you were given is not me, but why haven't you been able to figure it out?"

It was 4:00 a.m. when I awoke from the dream. I picked up the pad I kept on the nightstand and wrote down one word... 'Joan,' so I would recall my dream the next morning. At the first light of day, I headed to my favorite meditation chair. I closed my eyes began taking deep relaxing breaths. Mentally, I began repeating, "I'm ready to get an explanation about Joan." The first thought that came to me was that I had watched the *Joan of Arcadia* show the evening before, and perhaps, it had something to do with the actress that played Joan.

Go into the shed, and you'll find the answer as to why no one has been able to sculpt, paint, or get the true story or purpose of one called JOAN OF ARC, a voice that was firm but soft, directed me.

It's times like this that the only sound that comes out of my mouth is "DUH!"

I got out of the chair and headed for the storeroom. I finally located the painting, or what was left of it. The elements of frost, Texas heat, and mice had left the canvas in shreds. My first thought was, "Does this mean that I may have missed an opportunity to find out why I could never relate to the painting?"

After I got back to the house, I headed for my chair, closed my eyes, and mentally pleaded, "I'm ready to listen to an explanation… I'm ready to listen to an explanation." I kept repeating those words.

The following answer was given to me verbatim:

The one known as 'Joan of Arc' came into a physical body and was a vehicle for a host of many souls that expressed through her body. Each time a soul moved into her body for a temporary purpose, transfiguration took place. At that time in earth's history, the evolutionary process for souls that chose physical bodies to express an experience involved setting up scenarios that involve brutal and harsh treatment to their newly acquired physical bodies.

The one known as 'Joan of Arc' in actuality agreed to be that vehicle. Taking on the female character served a purpose showing that a female had capabilities as a warrior. The body was in constant use for disincarnate souls, and transfiguration was going on constantly, so which one was Joan of Arc? The answer is hundreds. It would be impossible to capture just one portrait and claim that it was Joan's, the true likeness. You were in a physical body with Joan before her mission began, so you saw her in a different light. Every so often, souls that express through a physical body make connections with one of their soul group and enjoy touching base. That is what happened. The artist was the channel. On this level of her awareness, she knew it was to be your painting. It was Joan's way of getting you to remember her.

61

Far fetched? Not really. All during this lifetime, I've had flashbacks of past experiences. At first, I did not understand. As I read, studied, and listened to my inner guidance, I learned to accept it, and it made sense. This one, however, was a bit unusual, as it took me so long to figure out what the portrait was all about.

But as I repeat to my students, "Everything is possible, even if at the time, there's no logical explanation. My suggestion is to pursue your dreams if they are persistent and important enough."

MEMORY OR IMAGINATION?

IT'S ONLY A DREAM, OR IS IT?

"Was it a memory or imagination?" I questioned when I read Art Linkletter's name on my dream notepad. I keep the pad handy to jot down my thoughts when I wake up during the night after a dream. A word or a phrase can help me interpret it the following morning.

After fixing my bowl of raisin bran, a bagel, and a pot of green tea, I sat at the kitchen table and made out my grocery list. This evening I'm venturing out to go grocery shopping. But last night, I had an out-of-body experience. Well, that's all I can call it. You weren't there, so don't play judge. (Just another compulsive disorder surfacing—being on the defensive when I read what others may be thinking.)

My ritual for interpreting dreams is to head for my favorite chair, adjust the recliner to a comfortable position, close my eyes, relax and repeat the word or phrase and meditate. This time it was just the name, 'Art Linkletter.' Why would he appear in my dream state? I met Mr. Linkletter forty-two years ago when I appeared on his TV show.

Our family won a trip to Disneyland, and after the vacation, my husband and children went back home to Texas. I stayed on an extra three days to visit with a friend that had recently moved to California. I wanted to see some live TV shows.

My friend acquired tickets for the various shows, including Linkletter's daytime show *House Party*.

That night before going to sleep, I played a mind game and saw myself talking to Mr. Linkletter. When I got into the studio the next morning, a long line had already formed, and I was last in line. After the ushers opened the doors to admit everyone, three of us at the end of the line were turned away. We were given tickets to another show that was being taped several doors down. A couple in front of me took their tickets and left. I, however, stayed and stood by the closed doors.

63

Five minutes later, the door opened, and an usher stuck out his head. When he saw me, he asked why I hadn't gone to the other show. "I came to see Art Linkletter," I replied.

"Wait a minute; I'll check and see if there's a vacant seat." When he returned, he grinned and said he found one empty seat and let me into the third row, third from the aisle.

When Mr. Linkletter came on stage, he announced that a member of the audience would be getting a Christmas gift from him. After he looked over the audience, he left the spotlight, and walked up the aisle steps, and stopped on the third row where I happened to be sitting. He waited a moment, looked directly at me, and then asked me to stand up. "You are about to receive a very special present," he grinned and then asked me to follow him to the spotlight.

A large box wrapped with a red bow was wheeled out from backstage, and I was to lift up the cover to open my present. When I did, a little person dressed in a Santa Claus costume jumped out, kissed me on the cheek, and presented me with a slim jewelry box, which contained a gold diamond-encrusted LeCoutre wristwatch. I stood there, blank and amazed at the unpredictable presentation. When I saw a large box, I thought I'd be getting a big size TV. Mr. Linkletter was amused at my response. "Surprised you didn't I?" he said as a flash of humor crossed his face.

Following the program, Mr. Linkletter approached me, cocking his eyebrow questioningly. He asked if we'd ever met before. I assured him that we had not. "But I know you," he insisted, as he stood making small talk while the show credits were displayed on the home viewer's screen. Are you sure we've never met? He again repeated. "Perhaps I remind you of someone you know," I explained, for I too had a feeling I knew him... but not sure from where or when. (This show was aired in 1963 on Christmas Day.)

When I finished mentally recalling the above episode, I began my ritual of finding the answer to... WHY NOW? by repeating the word I had jotted down the night before.

"Art Linkletter... Art Linkletter," I repeated aloud as I relaxed and waited for an answer. It took only a moment or two for pictures to appear in my mind's eye. The scene was a classroom. Students were dressed in white robes and sitting on the floor in a semicircle listening to a teacher repeating familiar phrases and proverbs and interpreting them.

I recognize Pat, my husband, Art Linkletter, my friends José Silva, Dr. Joseph Murphy, and Norman Vincent Peale in the group. *You continue to be instructed for your teaching assignment,* the teacher informed us. I began asking questions.

QUESTION: "My husband, José Silva, Dr. Joseph Murphy, and Norman Vincent Peale are no longer in the physical body, so why are they here with Mr. Linkletter and me?

The answer I got was something I needed to think about, so I wrote it down verbatim.

ANSWER: *Every person and all the events of your life are there because you have drawn them there. What you choose to do with them is up to you. The bond that links your true family is not one of blood but of respect and joy in each other's life. And meeting again, after years or lifetimes, is certain for those who are friends. The time, the place matters not.*

QUESTION: "Is Mr. Linkletter consciously aware of his dreams and that we knew each other, if not in this dimension, then in another?"

ANSWER: *He does not know you consciously, only on the inner plane. If you wish to share this experience with him, do so. The tape of the 1963 Christmas Day program may jog his memory of your meeting in the physical. His taped shows are available to him. How he responds to your making contact with him is his decision.*

As awareness of souls in physical bodies evolves, all will remember their friends and will be able to touch base in both dimensions. At this time, many people have this capacity but are reluctant to discuss it for fear of being ridiculed.

I had that dream on the night of February 8th, 2003. I have still not made the decision if I want to send Mr. Linkletter this experience.

It would be interesting to know if it means anything to him.

To my last question of WHY NOW? I got my answer…

Every now and then, it's fun touching base with friends in the here and hereafter.

To date, I have not contacted Mr. Linkletter. If our paths crossed while we were still in our physical bodies, I probably will share this incident with him.

The only reason for my sharing this story with you is… some of you that are reading this may have had a similar experience with a friend or one that has passed on. Perhaps this will help you understand that awareness will continue in this lifetime or past one if you established a bond with someone.

NOTE: Art Linkletter passed away a month before Helene did in 2010. I am sure they are together again.

JUST DOING HIS JOB

This morning I was getting ready to peel an orange and pick up a granola bar to go with my decaf when the phone rang. It was a friend that I occasionally played bridge with at the senior center.

She told me that last night, when she got home from her Bible class shortly after seven, she noticed, as they drove up to the house, that her bedroom light was on. She opened the front door and heard noises. She doesn't have a cat or dog and immediately flagged her friend, who had just dropped her off and was in the process of leaving, to stop.

She got her cell phone and called the police.

"We sat there for about ten minutes before they got there," she said, beginning to describe the events in detail. "Two policemen pulled out their guns and went into the house. After about ten minutes, they came out. They found no intruders, so I went in. I had to make a list of articles missing and file a report. The place was a mess. All the doors were pulled out of the closet, etc."

Luckily, she had homeowners insurance, and she is now considering a security system.

As I sat my recliner getting ready to share with you another chapter in my life, this incident surfaces:

My husband, Pat, was in the bathroom shaving, and I was getting ready to get out of bed to start my day when I saw a tall figure standing in the doorway. It startled me, but for some strange reason, I was not frightened. In a moment, I received this telepathic message, *Do not open the door today. Do not believe him if you request to use your phone. Your life is in danger.* The next moment the figure disappeared.

Our belief in guardian angels is a very ancient one, going all the way back to biblical times. These heavenly beings of beauty and light have long been thought to guide the footsteps—and the destiny—of those in their charge.

Saying the following prayer to my Guardian Angel and mentally repeating it before falling asleep at night brings peace, contentment, and a feeling of protection for me. I've done this since the age of six with my grandmother taught me the prayer.

Angel of God, My guardian dear…
To whom God's love commits me here
Ever this day be at my side…
To light, and guard, to rule and guide
Amen

Which brings me to the following story that happened, reinforcing my belief that I definitely am protected and that I do have a Guardian Angel.

I got up, put my robe on, and headed for the kitchen to begin fixing breakfast. I told Pat what just happened and dismissed it as my vivid imagination at work.

We had just moved into our new home in University Hills in Irving, Texas, a week earlier. Ours was the first home built in the pricey development. I won the house in a national contest sponsored by the Formica Corporation. For the past month, the house had been on display and opened to the public. After all the publicity and public relations representatives were gone, we settled in to enjoy the place.

Before Pat left for work that morning, he paused by the door and said, "This could just be your vivid imagination, but promise me that you will not open the door to anyone… we are isolated out here, and there's not much traffic… just be careful," he cautioned.

"I plan on staying home and arranging my books according to subject matter today, and I have no plans to go out… and no, I won't open the door today for anyone," I assured him.

Fifteen minutes later, Pat walked back into the house. With a forced grin, he said, "Before I got on the highway, I thought I heard someone say *go back home*. I guess you spooked me."

"Let's keep the drapes closed today. While you get your books organized, I'll catch up on my bookwork," he suggested. We didn't discuss 'what ifs.' In fact, I felt foolish mentioning the incident which caused him to stay home from work.

After lunch, I decided to go to the den and curl up with the latest Dean Koontz book. It was shortly after 3:00 p.m. when the shrill ring of the front doorbell brought me back to the NOW.

Pat, who was dozing in his recliner, jumped up, instantly wide awake. Another ring at the door got our attention.

"I'll look through the peephole to see who it is… you stay put," Pat suggested as he headed for the front of the house. In a few minutes, he returned. "It's a young guy, and I don't like his looks," he said. Another ring, this one, was long and louder as if someone was impatient.

"Let's go to the front bedroom so I can look out the window and see if there's a car on the street," he suggested. The windows were closed with heavy drapes. Pushing the drape aside about an inch so he could look out, he told me that there was a motorcycle parked out front.

For the next few minutes, Pat just stood by the window holding my son's bat, the only protection we had. I was silently praying that the person would leave. "There is another guy out there. He just came out from the side of the house, evidently waiting for the door to open so he could join his partner," Pat turned to me and said, "He's tall with long stringy black hair and an unshaven face… looks like a character out of a cop and robber movie. They're talking now." In a few minutes, I heard Pat heave a sigh of relief and say, "Thank God they are leaving. They are heading toward their motorcycle." In a few minutes, they spent away.

After we gained our composure, we hashed over some 'what ifs.'

What if they've broken down the door? What if I had opened the door? Did they have a gun, or did they just want to rob us? We will never know.

"This calls for a fresh pot of coffee," I suggested as I walked toward the kitchen. As I was measuring the coffee into the pot, I said aloud, "Thanks for the warning this morning." Then I heard a voice whisper in my ear, *just doing my job.*

By now, you should be convinced that when you hear a small voice or get a feeling about something being amiss… heed it.

And remember to give thanks to your unseen protectors.

I BELIEVE IN DESTINY

This is one of those days that I really miss my husband. I sort through yesterday's mail that lies beside my recliner while I have strawberry yogurt. I had company that came at noon yesterday and left late last night, and I didn't get around to opening the mail.

The letter was addressed to my precious husband, Pat. He was a member of the World War II Glider Pilots Association. Although I informed them of his death on February 12th, 2002, he still keeps getting notices of their reunions.

This morning seems a good time to share with you how we met.

"That's the man I'm going to marry," I confidently stated to my older sister and cousin when I saw the tall redheaded cadet standing by the doorway. We were at the community pavilion, where every Saturday night, there was a dance with a local band playing all the latest 'Hit Parade' songs.

It was 1943 when the seventy-two cadets came to Aberdeen, South Dakota, where I lived. The cadets were there to learn to fly and land gliders. The Dakota flat terrain was ideal for training.

My cousin turned to me and said, "He's not even good-looking."

"How about the dreamboat standing next to him? I could go for him 'big time.'"

A few seconds later, the cadet I had first noticed walked up to me and asked me to dance.

"Might as well," I flippantly shrugged my shoulders as I replied.

"Guess we should get acquainted because you and I are going to get married as the saying goes... will live happily ever after."

"I beg your pardon, young lady. Is this a joke?"

"No, I'm dead serious." *What on God's green earth made me blurt out such a statement?* It all happened so fast; I was dumbfounded that I should say something like that to a total stranger.

71

One might say it was love at first sight and touch because I got cold chills down my spine when we touched hands. I felt that it was much more—it was destiny for Helene (me) and Pat (the cadet) to meet and be together.

Pat was so serious. I guessed it was his upbringing. He was a Texan with a family background of teachers, ministers, judges, and lawyers.

One evening on a date together, he explained what volunteering to be a glider pilot meant. "It's a pilot program that the Air Force feels will be beneficial to our winning the war. I have no idea where I will be sent," he confided to me on a serious note.

I continued to assure him that it was not his destiny to die and he would return unharmed.

Two months later, he left South Dakota for more training in Kentucky. We wrote, and four months later, I received a letter telling me he would be going overseas. I didn't hear from him again for three months. His first letter told me that he was in India, four hundred miles behind Japanese lines, flying in supplies for the ground forces that were building the Burma Road. The first night when the lead planes unhooked the gliders to land their cargo, eight are the ten glider planes crashed, and six of the pilots were killed. Pat was not among them.

He was in India for eleven months before he went stateside.

As the Japanese moved in closer, the base was always under the threat of snipers. The snipers hid in the treetops; one sniper was so bold, he hid in the lister bag (a long, canvasback suspended from a tree limb that contained their drinking water.

"The only thing that kept my morale up was remembering how positive you were that it was not my destiny to die because we were to live happily ever after. The words 'happily ever after' would come to mind whenever I felt fear or was aware of impending danger," he told me upon his return.

After Pat was discharged, we were married. We raised three beautiful children in our 'happily ever after' togetherness spanned sixty years. Last year at the age of eighty-two, Pat left this dimension.

The years we shared together were crowded with exciting experiences. If history repeats itself, I know that we are destined to meet and be together again, so we continue sharing our love and adventures.

It gave me great comfort when one of his Glider Pilot Association buddies sent me the following poem written by Joyce Hill titled *On Silent Wings*. It was written as a tribute to all glider pilots.

So quiet was his approach that the Lord and Angels were unaware,
A Glider Pilot had met fate and was now standing at Heaven's gate.
"How could this happen? For unto ME is known all things," the Lord
explained.
The Glider Pilot's answer was, "Sir, I came on Silent Wings."

THE INCREDIBLE PAUL TWITCHELL

TRUSTING THE SOUL DIMENSION

"Today is the day that I'm going to get a book and read it," I said aloud as I looked out the window and stirred my oatmeal with fresh blueberries. I even splurged at the H-E-B bakery and got a cinnamon roll to go with my cup of green tea.

The book I was led to pull off the shelf for my collection of over six hundred was, *In My Soul I'm Free* by my special friend, Paul Twitchell. The following story illustrates the unique relationship we shared.

My friend Susan was a 'Metaphysical Butterfly.' Flitting from class to class, her enthusiasm was contagious. When she heard of a lecture or book about metaphysics or the occult, she pursued it briefly. She was searching for the answers about herself, life, and the universe. Trouble was, she didn't stay with anything long enough to see if it had merit. It was Susan who told me about Paul Twitchell. After she read his book, *The Tigers Fang*, she contacted Paul, asking him to come to Dallas and give a lecture on ECKANKAR: The Ancient Science of Soul Travel.

This was in early December of 1968 when I was interested in and studying metaphysical subjects. Susan told me she needed at least twenty people to form a class, and the charge would be $50 a person. "All Paul expects is to cover airfare, hotel, and a meeting place," she said.

No way I was going to pay that kind of money for a two-hour class period. Besides, I'd not read Twitchell's book, and just what was Eckankar anyway?

All Susan really knew about Paul Twitchell was from his book. When she talked to him, he told her that he was a very private person. He wanted to go directly to the hotel after she picked him up at the airport. He also directed her not to plan any social gatherings.

"I am coming to teach my philosophy Saturday morning and catching a plane after the class," he informed her. She was disappointed because she enjoyed having social gatherings, especially with anyone lecturing and teaching metaphysical subjects so she could 'pick his brain.'

I guess Paul had a change of plans that Saturday evening after Susan met his plane. My husband and I were in the den watching TV when the front doorbell rang.

"I wonder who is coming by so late. It's after 9:00 p.m." I commented as we both got up and walked to the front door to see who it was. I looked through the peephole and saw Susan standing with the man.

When I opened the door to let Paul Twitchell into my home and into my life, I learned so much. Apparitions, thought forms, and becoming invisible were but a few insights this Master shared with me.

The most outstanding feature about his 5' 6", well-dressed man wearing the traditional pressed shirt with a tie was his deep-set and penetrating celestial blue eyes.

I immediately remarked, "Did anyone ever tell you that when they look into your eyes, they can see forever?" Paul's smile brought an immediate softening to his features.

"I should have warned you; Helene tells it the way she sees it. She actually told one speaker to talk slower the first time she heard him lecture," Susan said to Paul as we walked toward the den.

"Did he talk slower?" Paul asked as a flash of humor crossed his face.

"He sure did. I was actually glad because I had a hard time understanding him too. He had such a heavy foreign accent."

"Anyone care for a coffee or snack?" I asked after everyone was seated in the den.

"Just tea for me," Paul answered.

Susan began telling Paul about my work with José Silva and what the program was about. My husband and Paul listened. I was trying to figure out who the barefooted, tall, smiling, brown-faced person was standing behind Paul's chair. His large black eyes were compelling, magnetic, filled with shifting stars. I started to fidget, moving about my chair, thinking the lights and shadows must be playing tricks in my eyes. Paul turned to me and asked, "Is something disturbing you?"

"Well, yes, my mind must be working overtime. I think I see a giant standing behind you." There was a trace of laughter in Paul's voice as he replied, "That's Rebazar Tarzs."

"And who in God's green earth is Rebazar Tarzs?"

"He is my teacher. He has his ashram in the Himalayans. If he bothers you, I'll tell him to leave."

I turned to my husband and asked, "Surely you can see him. Or Susan, can you see him?"

"No." They both replied as they looked to Paul for an explanation.

"It's not important if one cannot see in the Soul Dimension. They will feel a presence and many times get a message if they are sincerely seeking answers," Paul explained.

"The reason I came to meet you tonight is because I know you from the Soul Dimension, and I always enjoy making contact with people I've been with in the past."

"But I know absolutely nothing about Eckankar, and the Science of Soul Travel is completely foreign to me," I informed him. "I like your vibes, but I don't recognize you," I added.

He seemed to be far away for a moment as he explained. "My intention is not to gather followers. My purpose is to remind students what they know on a soul level. They will be guided and led to Eckankar to review what they forgot."

After Susan and Paul left that evening, my husband turned to me and said, "This guy is really sincere. I'd like to know more about him. Let's go to his program in the morning."

All I can tell you about what transpired during the two-hour class the following morning is that the information came from a soul level. We were all guided into another dimension. It's difficult to explain, so I won't even get into it.

"You will be hearing from me shortly," were Paul's parting words to me as we left. Driving home, my husband and I had a lot to talk about.

I thought Paul was just being polite when he said I would be hearing from him. The holidays are approaching, and Christmas was always a big family occasion, so I was occupied with those preparations.

It was New Year's Eve, and my husband and I were on our way home from Dallas, where we attended one of Susan's socials. The roads were slippery, visibility was poor, and the elevated bridge we were approaching was covered with a sheet of ice. An oncoming Corvette skidded into our car, and the next thing I realized was that I was drowning in my own blood. The only thing I thought about was a technique I learned in Mind Control. I heard someone say, "You can stop the bleeding."

At this time, there's no need to go into details about my learning experience. I had a remarkable recovery. I wrote about it in my book, *The Name It & Claim It Game.*

The morning after the accident, while I was in the hospital, a letter arrived in the mail at home. It was a personal note from Paul. All he said was, "The night I was at your home, I was aware of the automobile accident you were to experience. It was already in motion, and there was nothing I could do to stop it. You will be fine," Paul wrote.

One year later, my second meeting with Paul was in Las Vegas. I was attending a class with Dr. William J. Bryan Jr., president of the American Institute of Hypnosis on Body Language. Susan was attending the worldwide Eckankar seminar. Susan and I roomed together. We had a lot to talk about in the evening after our meetings.

Paul called my room when he heard I was in Vegas. He said he had someone I should meet. We met in a dining room that evening, and he introduced me to Brad Steiger. Brad was writing Paul's biography titled, *In My Soul, I Am Free*, which was published in 1968. Over the years, I ran into Brad frequently. We were speakers at the same seminars. To date, Brad has written over one hundred books about people that experienced other dimensions. After Brad excused himself, Paul and I sat down with some tea to 'catch up,' especially about the time he appeared to me in his 'light body' (as he called it) one morning 'just to talk.'

"I took on the assignment to make you aware that you will be called upon to help, encourage and explain situations to people that are not yet aware," he explained during our meeting in Vegas.

The following year I had numerous occasions when Paul would simply appear. It was a mental exchange, but it was as if he were in the same room with me. How I wish that my husband and Susan could have experienced him in his 'light body.'

On one of the occasions that Paul appeared, he told me that before the day was up, I was to tell someone that when they heard a voice, saw or felt the presence, they were to discern, discern, discern. I was to inform them that they were pranksters in the unseen world that played tricks on naive vulnerable people. For some people that were deeply religious, the Virgin Mary would appear and tell them something they were to do. To caution the person that an apparition coming from a higher intelligence would NEVER tell anyone what they were to do. In the fourth dimension, there's a lot of illusion taking place. Many times, it is a combination of a thought form that was created and is used as an excuse for an issue they were not able to face at the time. "This is what is happening to the person you will be making contact with today," he said before vanishing.

I had no phone calls during the day, nor did I feel inclined to call anyone. When my husband got in from work that evening, I told him verbatim what Paul discussed that morning. I suggested that we go visit his elderly mother, who lived fifty miles from us. I felt she was lonesome. Somehow I didn't think the message was meant for his mother. Perhaps, was meant for Bonnie, the University student that was given a free room and breakfast, so my husband's mother would not be alone at night.

Many times while visiting his mother, Bonnie would be there. We got to know her quite well. I assumed if she was there and we talked, the conversation might lead to something where I could share the suggestion that she should be more discerning. She wasn't there when we arrived at 7:00 p.m. I kept stalling to leave as it was almost 10:00 p.m., and we had an hour's drive ahead of us to get home. She finally popped in, but only for a minute to get something. She said she was going up to get a pizza with friends and would be back later. I was disappointed.

Driving home, I was trying to figure out what happened.

"Maybe we should've stayed until Bonnie got back," I said to my husband as he was making a turn off the main highway towards home. That's when I noticed the shopping center where a couple I met at one of my lectures said their barbecue cafe was located.

"Turn in here," I excitedly directed. "I have an invitation to stop for coffee with the young couple that own that cafe."

"The whole shopping strip is closed. There isn't a light on anywhere," my husband said.

"Go to the back. They are there. It doesn't matter if it's almost 11:00 p.m. I KNOW they are still there."

There was a car parked by the back door of the cafe. When we knocked, and they answered, I heaved a sigh of relief. I KNEW that this couple was to be the recipients of Paul's message.

As we sat having coffee, I casually asked, "Do you guys know Eckankar? I met Paul Twitchell, the founder of the program. He is most interesting and tuned in. Paul told me something that I will never forget."

They had never heard of Eckankar or Paul.

I then began repeating verbatim what Paul had said earlier that morning.

As I was talking, I noticed the couple look over at each other. She hung her head and began fidgeting with a locket on a chain she was wearing, but neither said a word. We thanked him for coffee and got up to leave. The young man let us through the kitchen to the back door. As we passed the fridge, he opened it and handed me a five-pound package of baby back ribs.

"Do you have any idea what just happened? Someone must have sent you. My wife thinks she's been getting messages from the Virgin Mary telling her to leave me, that sex was dirty, and a lot of other gibberish that's turning her against me."

"She would not believe me, but when you told her, I could see it made sense to her. She's great admiration for you since we heard you lecture several months ago."

"WOW!" was all I could say is we were driving home. Today I KNOW what to say, when to say it, and to whom to say it. I learned my lesson well, thanks to Paul's help.

Becoming Invisible

Let's go back to that night in Las Vegas. After Brad left, Paul and I began exchanging experiences, but his students constantly interrupted us. Someone wanted Paul to autograph their books; some just wanted to talk about his classwork. It was becoming a nuisance.

"Let's go to my room to continue this conversation," I suggested.

"I have a better idea," Paul said in a casually jesting way, "Let's become invisible."

"You've got to be kidding—well, maybe not," I added when I recalled reading the book, *Psychic Discoveries Behind the Iron Curtain*. The authors wrote about the famous Wolf Messing who was sought after by Hitler to spy on other countries during the war. They were never able to capture him. It was said that Messing could become invisible at will.

"Will it kid, and it will happen," is the only direction Paul gave me. For the next hour or so while we were talking, we had no further interruptions.

Before leaving, I asked him to explain how it worked.

"You are using the power of concentration already, so this small feat should be easy for you."

He was right. I had to use it constantly during the two and a half months I was on assignment in Peru. I'll share more of that exciting story with you later in this book.

The next time I met Paul in the physical was when he was invited back to Dallas to give a seminar for his students. I was not able to attend. José Silva was in town teaching, and I was still working with him.

That evening, Susan called me at home and said that Paul would like to see me. "Can I bring over some friends?" she asked.

"Sure." After seven of the students, Susan, and Paul arrived, they gathered in the den. Paul called me aside and asked if he could talk in private. I let him to my office.

"I'm so exhausted, I just want to rest," he said as he eased his body into the king-sized recliner I use in my office. In a minute, his eyes closed. I covered him with an afghan and left the room to join Susan's friends. I was anxious to hear what had transpired at the seminar. They were disappointed that Paul did not join them, but soon they were caught up in sharing their experiences, and everyone was having a good time.

Several hours later, I looked in on Paul. He sat up when he heard the door open. We talked briefly as it was getting late. I recall our conversation as if it was happening now.

"My time here on this plane is going to an end. You know, I'm looking forward to leaving this body."

"What about Eckankar, who will take over?"

"That will be up to higher intelligence. They will present the opportunity to someone who is presently a student. Changes will be made over the years as each person who takes on the responsibility will have his own ideas he wishes to express." He sighed as if a great burden had suddenly been lifted.

That was our last meeting. My responsibility working with José and the beginning of lecturing as a free agent began. Paul made his transition four months later while he was conducting a seminar.

That's life. People come and go. As we encounter new faces and places, our learning experiences continue. Over the years, I have been blessed to meet many special beautiful people. Paul Twitchell was one of them.

I never will believe my meeting Paul was an accident. I learned so much from him.

ADVICE: Realize that if you are open, every person you meet will be able to teach you something.

MY DEAR FRIEND JOSÉ

A MAN BEYOND ORDINARY UNDERSTANDING

Before having breakfast this morning, I decided to check my emails. There was a reminder on the screen that the 40th Silva Mind Control Convention would be held in Laredo, Texas, again in August, as it is every year.

I've already had several phone calls from friends asking if I plan on attending. I have too many commitments, and I'm not keen on traveling in all this Texas heat. But you simply must let me share with you how I first met this remarkable man.

I learned so much from this beautiful man, as I'm sure the millions of students who took his classes did. The program is still being taught all over the world.

A Man With a Message and a Method

"You must come to Fort Worth with me to hear a man from Laredo," Susan, my Metaphysical Butterfly friend, ordered in her authoritative voice. "He is giving a *free* introductory lecture on a program he calls The Silva Method of Mind Control. I heard he was in Amarillo last week, and I got word that he's a <u>must</u> to meet and hear."

I'm eternally grateful to Susan for prompting me to attend this lecture about Mind Control. It wasn't about controlling someone else's mind. It was about controlling your own mind. The man, José Silva, not only had a message, he had the method for each of us to find our own answers. After hearing José, I knew I had to learn more about this program.

When José stepped to the platform in front of a crowded room that Sunday afternoon, I got the impression that he was not interested in the unimportant things of life. He was a man meant for heroism. In the 1970s, one had to be determined and independently minded enough to buck the flak from people whose mindsets were fixed. Although I felt that organized religions in the scientific community

85

were his biggest opposition, José's attitude was, "They will see the merit one day how the mind and our thinking control our lives. I must continue to teach Mind Control to all who will listen," he explained.

He began by explaining how our brain functions and referred to the color charts that made it easy for me to follow and understand. The only difficulty I had was trying to comprehend every word. He had a thick accent and spoke too fast. I remedied that during the first break when I approached him and suggested he speak slower. He thanked me for the suggestion and continued in a more unhurried pace.

You must get to know this man better, a small voice in my head repeated when he completed the presentation and began asking the audience if anyone had any questions.

When everyone was finished with their questions, I stood up and said, "I have one last question—how would you like to come to my house in Irving and join my friends for dinner this evening?" Everyone laughed as he replied, "Thank you, I would be honored."

After Jan, Barbara, Ann, and I got into Susan's Lincoln and were on our way home, Susan said, "I'm so glad you asked him. Now we can pick his brain some more."

When we arrived at my place, Susan, Jan, Ann sat in the den and talked to my husband. Barbara and I headed for the kitchen to fix something to eat. I prepared my easy casserole with tuna, cashews, chips, mushroom soup, and grated cheese and popped it in the oven to bake. Barbara cleaned and arranged a tray of raw vegetables.

We ate after José arrived and then sat in the den and listened to him talk until midnight. Tomorrow was a workday for the girls, so they had to leave. Before leaving, Susan, Jan, and I offered to help José set up a lecture in Dallas. Barbara and Ann said they would help whenever they could, but since they were both airline stewardesses, their schedules would be more restrictive.

The next day, José left to go back to Laredo. Susan, Jan, and I got busy the next evening via the telephone, contacting Susan's metaphysical and meditation friends. We had over sixty people attend the introductory lecture. Thirty-four signed up to take his first class in Dallas. Each time José came to town, he presented an introductory lecture and follow with a class. We were kept busy.

After four months of organizing programs and having weekly meetings in my home that we called a Cottage Group, Susan and Jan could no longer help me. Susan was given more responsibility at her job and did a lot of evening work; Jan began traveling for the company she worked for. That left me on my own.

I became José's secretary and PR person—a huge undertaking for this then stay-at-home mom. Soon I realized it was getting a lot of help from other dimensions—what a FUNtastic learning experience.

Every time José came to teach a class, I had him join my husband and me for dinner. I called it our 'catch-up time.'

Following the introductory lecture, José offered a class that he taught in three phases. After each two-day class, he encouraged us to practice before we continued to the next level of training. That's why I started the Cottage Group.

Bear with me as I digressed for a moment. When I met Dr. Joseph Murphy, a Catholic priest, writer, lecturer, and author of over thirty books, one of which is *The Power of Your Subconscious Mind*, I kidded him about using the same antidotes and the many articles and books he had written. His answer to me was, "Sometimes people have to read or hear something forty-two times before it registers."

José was well aware of this. That is why he encouraged mind control graduates to repeat his classes often as they chose.

Graduates of the program receive a card that can be presented in any city or country to meet other Mind Control instructors. They can repeat the classes anywhere it is taught. Today, classes are taught in 109 countries.

NOTE: You can now learn online from anywhere in the world via The Silva Method website. https://silvamethod.com/

José began his research in brain wave control in brain wave control in Laredo, Texas in 1944. He began teaching in the fall of 1969.

Every time José came to Dallas to teach, he would bring me books that he found interesting. "We will talk about them the next time I come," he would say. Laura Huxley's *You Are Not The Target*, W. Grey Walters *The Living Brain*, and Shafica Karagulla's *Breakthrough to Creativity* were just a few of the books that we discussed.

We soon discovered I was good at sending the messages, and José was an excellent receiver. After word spread about his teachings, he was invited to Austin, San Antonio, Houston, and other places in Texas. I could not keep up with his schedule, where he was, or where he could be reached. Cell phones were not available at that time.

There were many occasions I needed to reach him to come early for a TV show or an interview for the local papers. He was now making news, and people were investigating his teachings. That is when I use telepathy to contact him. Within an hour, he would be calling me on the telephone to ask me what I wanted.

Soon there were so many requests for José to lecture; he began an instructor's training class, so his message and methods could reach more people.

One evening, about seven months after he began teaching in Dallas, José approached me with the sense of conviction I soon realized was part of his astrological Leo character and announced, "They tell me that you are going to go to Chicago and open up that area so I can go and teach there."

My response was immediate, "Not me. I do not like flying, and I have no idea where to start, so you can get somebody else to do that job." My vexation was evident.

José straightened himself with dignity. His expression stilled and grew serious, and all he said was, "We will talk about it later."

I knew what "We would talk about it later." meant. My husband and I used that phrase with the children over the years. To use it implied 'subject closed.'

That evening when my husband came home from work, I was still upset thinking about what José had asked.

"Would you believe that José thinks I'm going to go Chicago to open up that area for him to teach? You know how I hate to fly, and I would not know where to begin. I told him just to get somebody else to do it."

"How many times have you sat through his classes and listened to his techniques?" my husband patiently asked. He knew I attended every class when José was in town. It was my job to be there. I must have been more than ten times since meeting José.

"What's that got to do with it?" I replied, sharply disappointed because I was expecting some support from him.

"A lot." He explained. "Why don't you practice what you've been taught and find a solution? And by the way, it's time that you get over your fear of flying," he grinned mysteriously.

My childish side surfaced, so I dropped the issue and began setting the table. I gave it some serious thought the rest of the evening— OK, I was pouting—but it did not bring up the subject again.

The next morning I headed for my favorite chair to get serious about how I could find a solution. I know that you're probably thinking at this point, "She told us that Mind Control helped her find answers, so why isn't she using it?"

Good question… I do not have an answer for everything, but for this question, my excuse is, I was just not thinking. I jumped into the 'pity party' mood and was frightened about the big-time responsibility. Where to begin? What hotel to choose? What about advertising?

As I told you earlier, I'd been a stay-at-home mom for the past twenty-nine years and relied on my husband to make the decisions. Now he was telling me to make this decision by myself. I felt abandoned, afraid, and hurt.

Today, as I reflect back to that time, I realized that my precious husband was encouraging me to become independent and assertive, to make choices for myself.

What happened next was nothing short of a miracle.

"Somebody, somewhere has got to help me about the Chicago assignment," I repeated that phrase aloud, with intensity and determination almost ten times before…

The loud ringing of the telephone brought me back to the NOW. "I've got my answer, I've got my answer," I repeated as I headed to answer the call. I expected José to tell me that he found someone else to go to Chicago.

WRONG!

"Is this Mrs. Hadsell?" the voice on the line asked.

"This is she," I replied.

"You don't know me," she said. "My name is Mary Green, and I live in Chicago. I just read an article about your success in entering contests and winning all those prizes. Your story in this month's 'The Woman' magazine, but I'm not interested in contesting."

She continued, "I want to know more about The Silva Method that was mentioned in the article and where I can take the class? I'm fascinated how you were able to use the techniques for accelerated healing after your automobile accident."

After she paused, waiting for my answer, I realized that this was Opportunity opening a door. I composed myself and, in a professional voice, replied, "Mary, I'm supposed to come to Chicago to open the area so the Silva Method of Mind Control classes can be offered. I have to find a suitable meeting place, put an advertisement in the paper and arrange for a date."

"Oh, you don't have to come. I'll do all that for you. I am in public relations for a major shoe company. I know the hotels—I will get you reasonable rates and put ads in the paper." Her enthusiasm was evident, and she continued, "I'll even get your hotel rooms free and pick you up at the airport."

I stood there, blank, amazed, and shaken as she continued.

"Oh yes, and I'm a member of the Unity Church. This congregation is one of the few open-minded groups I have met since moving here three years ago. When I tell them that The Silva Method will give an introductory lecture, I'm sure we can fill the hall."

She only stopped long enough to catch her breath, and I took the opportunity to offer, "I'll send a check for the room deposit in the advertisement if you just let me know how much it is."

"No need to do that; we can take care of that when you get here." After getting her address and telephone number, I thanked her and hung up.

I was so excited, relieved, and surprised that I called my husband at his office. I never contacted José until all the arrangements for the Chicago opening were complete.

Do you know what José said? "Higher intelligence told me that you would be getting their help. And, by the way, you should go to Chicago and overcome your fear of flying. There was much work ahead that requires flying." I got the impression after he hung up the telephone that he exhaled a long sigh of contentment and thanked higher intelligence.

Harry McKnight, one of the instructors, was sent to Chicago to open and teach the class. I also went. José planned to follow and teach classes at a later date. Mary did a superb job. She became secretary of the area, helping Harry until José conducted his classes. Thank heaven I did not have to go again…

I'm not going to tell you that I immediately lost the fear of flying because I did not. I used every mind trick that I knew to con myself.

I was relieved that the Chicago opening was over. I was now again content to stay in Texas.

Alas, that did not last long. Two months later, José again approached me. This time he told me that I was to open the Detroit area.

"Hey, wait a minute," I declared. "Haven't you been reading the papers? They are rioting in the streets, and they have a 10:00 p.m. curfew."

He regarded me quizzically for a moment and replied, "They tell me the time is now, so it must be done."

Of course, my first thought after he told me it was, *Will I get another telephone call that will come to my rescue and will do all the preliminary work, so I have to go?*

But it did not happen that way. That very evening as I was taking registrations from people that were signing up to take the class, a graduate asked me if José still offered scholarships to nuns and priests.

"Of course," I replied.

"My cousin is a priest from Detroit and is visiting me. He came with me tonight in hopes he could take the class after I told him about it," she explained.

The thought that the help I needed was already done deal made me want to shout. "Thank you… Thank you, Higher Intelligence."

During the first break, I offered the priest coffee and cookies and told him that José was ready to go to Detroit to teach classes. And that it was my job to the advance preparations. I did not even have to ask for his help. He was so enthused; he volunteered to get the hall, place the ads, and invite his church members to the introductory lecture.

I could write several books on the 'miracles' that happened while I worked for José. Higher intelligence was always there. I never cease to be amazed. When José and I discussed it, he responded by saying, "The programs offer an opportunity for people that are ready to have a raise in consciousness. I am only the facilitator; the ones that are ready and take the classes are reminded that they are responsible for their thoughts. The visual charts show current scientific research on how the mind and brain work. Higher intelligence is helping and encouraging us for our evolutionary process."

José was right about my flying. For the next twenty-five years, I traveled all over the world on assignments. Today I feel safer in a plane than I do in a car.

If you ask me today what the one most significant thing I learned from José was, it would have to be this. If you want to be of service to your fellow man, be open to contact other realms so they can help you. You are, I'm sure, familiar with the phrase, Ask, and you shall receive. Seek, and you shall find. Knock, and the door will open.

A simple phrase I repeat to this day when I lecture, write, or counsel people is, "Let me be a channel to help people help themselves." Then I sit back and let things happen.

Before closing this chapter, there's an incident I am led to share with you. It happened while José was in Dallas.

One of the students in the class was a manager of fast food restaurant. That Sunday night after class, the manager went directly to his place of business to count his weekend receipts for the Monday deposit. (This was at a time when places closed at 10:00 p.m.)

He found the office safe had been pried open and was empty. He called the man he had left in charge and was told that he indeed locked the safe. In fact, another employee had been present when they closed. Next, he called me in a panic and requested I call José immediately ask him who stole the money.

"Boy, if he can tell me who did it, I'll get the police and have the person arrested. Think of all the publicity. José will get."

"I'm pretty sure. I know who the thief is," he told me when I asked him if he had any idea who it might be. "I hired a cook two weeks ago, and for some reason, I don't trust him. I'll bet he's the one who stole the money."

I contacted José and told him what had happened. José's solution to everything that came up while I worked with him always surprised me.

"We don't need to prove we are psychics, nor do we need any publicity. We need to help right a wrong for this situation. Get in touch with your Cottage Group and tell them to project this to the thief. 'The money you took does not rightfully belong to you. Please return it.' I, too, will be projecting for its return," he assured me.

I had an agreement with the students that attended the weekly Cottage Group sessions that whenever there was an emergency, we would contact each other for support. The twenty or more people would send healing energy or telepathic messages if necessary.

I got busy on the telephone and called three people. They, in turn, called others until everyone in the group was contacted. Then I called the manager and told him what José suggested. I also told him to mentally contact the thief and ask him to return the money. He sounded disappointed but promised he would not call the police until the following morning.

Monday morning at 8:00 a.m., I had the call that made my day. It was the manager, "Mrs. Hadsell, I just arrived to open the store. I always use the back entrance, and when I open the screen door, two brown paper sacks full of money were between the doors. The amount of money was more than we usually take in on the weekends. How did José know that this would happen?"

"You're going to have to ask him when he comes to teach the next class."

When we hung up, I contacted José and the Cottage Group to tell them the good news. The manager still thought the cook was the thief. However, the cook was at his shift the same morning and acted as if nothing happened. Our project was to have the money returned, and it was accomplished.

There are many valuable phrases and words that all Silva Mind Control Method graduates practice in their daily learning experiences. One attribute of Mind Control graduates as they never accept a limitation as a problem. It is simply a project that is waiting to be solved. A phrase you will often hear from students is, "CANCEL! CANCEL!" when they say, think or hear anything negative. In addition, you will know you're with Mind Control graduate when you ask them, "How are you?" Their reply invariably, "Better and better!"

The relationship José and I shared spanned more than a thirty-year period. During this time, José and I touched base to chat every two months until he made his transition on February 7th, 1999. He was 85-years-old. This humble, dedicated soul touched so many lives with his wisdom that today his work lives on through his children, his books, and tapes.

Wherever you are, José, I want to thank you again for being a channel to help people to help themselves. Your assignment this lifetime has raised the consciousness of millions and has helped me to better understand my place in the universe.

Reflecting back, as I share my beautiful experience with José, my only regret is that all of you did not get to know him as I did. Since his transition, José and I have connected two times on the inner planes. His work continues.

CREATING THOUGHT FORMS

DON'T TAKE MY WORD FOR IT,
EXPERIENCE IT FOR YOURSELF

Every Wednesday, Sylvia Brown is on the Montel Williams talk show, a popular place where people in the audience can ask Sylvia about their departed loved ones and about the strange psychic experiences they have had.

I, too, have had a number of questions about the psychic and was searching for answers about my far-out experience as a child. I was searching for some kind of proof. That's what led me to England, but let me tell you how it all came about.

I'm not having breakfast this morning. I am going to a Toastmasters meeting today, and I'll have lunch with my peers.

TIME: May 18th, 1971
PLACE: London, England

After my husband dropped me off at the Spiritualist Association of Great Britain (SAGB) on 33 Belgrave Square, I opened the DOOR and my MIND to a new experience. I was there to listen and talk to dead people.

NOTE: The current address of the SAGB is 341 Queenstown Road, Battersea. https://sagb.org.uk/

When I told my husband I would like to go back to England for our three-week vacation, I had one motive, to visit the Spiritualist Association of Great Britain. My husband was not interested in listening to or talking to dead people. He was looking forward to studying architecture, visiting museums and libraries.

My adventurous nature wanted to investigate and do some serious research. We had been in England a year earlier with a tour group but had only been there for a two-day stay.

I hope that you are interested in joining me on my adventure.

I learned long ago to never try to prove anything to anyone—just let them experience it for themselves. I will, however, share my concepts for your consideration.

I had called the Spiritualist Association earlier that morning, and they told me the doors opened at 1:00 p.m. for public services (sometimes called Message Services). The mediums would begin their services at 2:00 p.m.

There were several people standing at a desk registering when I arrived shortly after 1:00 p.m. When it was my turn, the clerk looked up briefly and asked, "What medium do you want to sit with, or do you want a private message service?"

"This is my first time. What would you suggest?"

"Margaret, in room six, upstairs, is a good place to start. The service starts at 2:00 p.m. The donation is £2, and it lasts a half hour. There is a tea room in the basement that is a good place to wait," she suggested as she handed me my admission ticket for the service.

The tea room was not too fashionable, but it was already busy. People were chatting, drinking tea, and nibbling on biscuits (cookies).

I got a cup of tea at the counter and chose the table in the corner by myself. It didn't take long before the place was crowded. A short chubby woman asked if she could sit at my table.

"Did you come to talk to the dearly departed loved one?" she asked when she heard I was from Texas.

"This is all new for me. I don't know what to expect. Guess I'll just wait to see what happens."

Suddenly I heard a bell ringing. "It's time to go upstairs for the service," my newfound friend informed me. She was joining another group, so we parted.

The rooms were all on the second floor, where the mediums held services. Posted by the entrance of each numbered door was the name of the medium. I counted fifteen people in the room. Later I learned that the regulars often had their favorite medium, and some mediums had as many as thirty people in their service.

I decided to sit in on each of the mediums while I was in London.

Some mediums were more advanced, according to comments I overheard. I didn't want to miss anything, and this place was within walking distance from the hotel, so it was very convenient.

After everyone sat in a semicircle, the lights were dimmed, and the medium said a prayer before she began.

"There is a Betty that has a message for someone. Is there anyone present that has a loved one named Betty?" she asked.

A small man with grey hair that sat two seats from me replied, "She is my wife."

The medium began with the message, "She is near you. She tells me that she made many friends on the other side and for you not to fret. She's happy and loves you."

I watched to see the reaction of the man. He seemed content and peaceful as he said, "Thank you."

The medium then called out another name and received a response from a tall, thin woman dressed in navy. She wore a hat, which reminded me of a lampshade. Her eyes were so sad. She began to sob softly after she heard the message from her daughter. I noticed that all the people present were in their sixties or older. I was forty-seven at the time.

I did hear a name I recognized. It was the name of a deceased aunt, but I did not respond. When there was no response to the name recognition, the medium moved on and called out another name.

Before I left the building, I asked one of the ladies what medium she would recommend because I planned to attend again the next day. "Sarah has been there the longest. She's pretty good." So tomorrow I'd check out Sarah. I was not impressed with Margaret.

My opinion of the first day was… *just because they're dead does not mean they are smart*. Moreover, much of what the medium said sounded like a 'cosmic sermon.'

As soon as I arrived the next day, I headed for the tea room and was drawn to a woman wearing a bright purple sweater. Her face was pink with eagerness, and her hair looked like a silvery white cobweb. She fascinated me, so I approached her.

"I'm on vacation, and I heard about this place. I wanted to see it for myself. May I join you?" I asked. "I am a good listener and always take an interest in people's opinions."

She invited me to sit down and was eager to share her experiences with me. She told me her name was Mannie.

"I come here quite often, especially on our marriage anniversary. My husband passed away three years ago, but we still communicate." Her eyes gleamed with enthusiasm and anticipation.

"Some people come every month, and some come more often. I do not have that need," she probably said. "I know when he wants to make contact."

"What did he tell you?" I questioned, genuinely interested.

"Before his passing, he promised me that he would be waiting for me on the other side. He planted a rose bush in the backyard a year earlier when he first got sick," she explained. "He told me that on every anniversary, he would see to it that the bush would be alive and full blooms of red roses. That would be his message." Her thoughts momentarily were filtering back to that day. "The roses are blooming. The bush is loaded," she added.

"That is truly remarkable."

"If you like, I'll take you home with me to show you the bush," she offered.

"Thank you. That won't be necessary. I believe you. There are so many things I know nothing about, but I'm willing to learn."

"Come sit on Rose Ann's service with me. She's the best one of the lot." Before I could respond, she continued, "Better get your ticket now because they allow just so many in a room."

Rose Ann had an air of confidence when she walked into the room and sat in her chair. She smiled and folded her hands in a comfortable gesture and waited for all of the twenty-seven chairs to become occupied before she began. She told us that some of our loved ones would make their appearance in the room and that some of us would be able to see them or feel their presence. Her voice had an unusually pleasant resonance.

"We have a Joshua here. He tells me his family and friends called him Josh. He is a message for his wife." I looked over to my newfound friend seated beside me when she answered, "I'm here."

Josh's message was short. "The rose bush is in bloom for you, my love. The electric bill is wrong. Call the office and have them check the meter again." She nodded with a satisfied look.

Then I saw a figure standing behind the medium. A small man in stature, but I got the impression he carried himself with a commanding air of self-confidence. When I saw a pipe in his mouth and a cloud of smoke hovering over his head, I stammered softly with bewilderment, "My God, he is in the room beside the medium."

"I know," Mannie turned to me and smiled.

The rest of the contacts that day made no significant impression. I was too anxious to talk to Mannie. As we walked down the stairs towards the tea room, I was acutely aware of how proud she was as she straightened herself with dignity.

I ushered Mannie to a corner table. I had so many questions that needed answers. "You saw your husband behind the medium, too, didn't you? Was he smoking? I thought I saw smoke."

"He always had that pipe in his mouth. I got to where I liked the smell of smoke. You know, he had the tobacconist mix a special blend for him," she explained with intense pleasure.

"Does anyone else in your family make contact with you?"

"No, but my neighbor that died last year made contact two months after she passed. I really miss her, but I haven't heard since."

Just then, a woman came over to our table and asked, "Did Josh make contact today?"

"Yes, he did, and my roses are in full bloom today." Mannie then told the woman about the advice she got concerning the electric bill. The woman patted her arm and said, "Such a good man you had."

Before Mannie and I parted, she said I should have a private meeting with Rose Ann. "It will cost more, and be sure to have a list of questions you want answered," she suggested.

That evening, after I returned to my hotel and I shared what happened with my husband, he became interested. "Perhaps I *should* sit in on one of the services."

After giving it some more thought, he added, "She really must have a lot of energy to pull that off."

"What do you mean—the medium or the woman?"

"When you figure it out, let me know. Did you smell the smoke?" he asked.

I have a habit of carrying a notepad with me at all times, so I can jot down unusual happenings. This was a phenomenon worth recording. No, I had not smelled the smoke.

I had difficulty falling asleep that night. Ceaseless inward questions made me toss and turn. "Someone has an answer for what I saw today," I said aloud before getting comfortable enough to get some rest.

I awoke the next morning as my husband was opening the door to leave. "I thought I'd let you sleep in this morning. I'm going to get some breakfast and read the paper in the lobby," he said before closing the door.

He had met a tourist in the lobby the day before, and they were going to do some exploring together. I was pleased that he was enjoying himself. I certainly was.

I couldn't go back to sleep, so I got up and decided to peel an orange and skip the breakfast downstairs. The traffic below my window transmitted an even, steady sound. The passing of so many cars, blending in a deep harmonious hum, was hypnotic. I began daydreaming.

When I get inside my own head, travel time between now and then evaporates. My mind went back to an incident that happened while working with José Silva.

It was after class one night when one of the students, a six-foot-plus, over two-hundred-fifty pound attorney, asked if he could talk to José in private. José told him that I was to be included. Inform the attorney that we would all learn something from this meeting. "Anything discussed will be kept confidential," he assured the attorney.

"This may sound childish, but I'm afraid of the dark—almost to the point of being paranoid. I can't sleep unless the overhead light is on. When I go out at night and come home after dark, I have to check all the closets and under the bed until I'm convinced that there's no one in the house." The attorney awkwardly cleared his throat, searching for a plausible explanation.

"How long have you had this fear?" José asked.

"It started as a child."

"Can you describe what it is you see and fear?"

"Well, this is stupid, but it's a monster. He must be at least nine feet tall with sharp teeth, and... " he paused, stirring uneasily in his chair.

"With warts on his face and hands and green sticky fluid running down his mouth," José finished describing the monster while the stunned attorney sat and listened.

"Do you see him too?" he stammered.

"I sure do. You created a thought-form. It probably began as a child when you heard the expression 'the boogeyman will get you if you are not good or do not fall asleep.' Your imagination took over, and you created a creature with features that repulse you. Over time, you increasingly gave it more energy. It can't hurt you physically, but if you keep giving it energy with fear, it can psychologically affect your well-being," José explained softly with deep concern.

"Let's get rid of him now," José suggested as he turned to me and asked if I too saw the monster in the corner.

So fascinated by what I just heard, I gulped and weakly replied, "Yes, that thing is even frighting me."

"Let's gather energy, point our index finger at the monster, and demand that he get smaller and smaller."

The attorney and I followed José's directions. Can you picture the scene? Three grown adults, pointing our fingers at a thought-form and watching it shrink before our eyes.

When it was six inches high, José reached over, picked it up, and put it in the palm of his hand. "Do you still fear this doll? We can make it disappear completely, or we can leave it at that size. When fear surfaces again, you can see that he's only this small and can't hurt you," José explained as I watched the tense lines of the attorney's face relaxed in wonder.

"You mean I created that monster without knowing it?"

"Imagination is real for many people. When one thinks about something long and strong enough, they give it energy. They can actually see it. Many times others can also say it. This is what is known as a thought-form."

The grateful, bewildered attorney just shook his head, repeating, "What a relief. What a relief! How can I thank you?"

"You will learn more about this in class. When you finish the program, you will be able to control your mind and what you are thinking," José then went on to explain that creating thought-forms is something many people do when they grieve a loved one or are lonely. It comforts them, and many times it is harmless.

Deeply religious people see angels. Sometimes angels are thought forms, sometimes apparitions. The circumstances of each situation must be evaluated before determining which.

After mentally reviewing yesterday's incident, my logical mind kicked in as I began rationalizing what I witnessed yesterday. The medium gave the name Joshua, and she said that family and friends call him Josh. How does one explain that?

WHAT IF the medium, Rose Ann, was good at receiving messages that were projected by a good sender, namely Mannie?

WHAT IF the sender, Mannie, could also create a thought-form that resembles Josh as she remembered him, even down to the pipe you smoke?

WHAT IF Mannie did not know she was the creator and director of yesterday's episode, including the electric bill incident? She may have already questioned the charge before she came. In the past, did she rely on Josh to make decisions, and now she needed his opinion to agree with her?

WHAT IF the medium, Rose Ann, was merely the mediator and thought she was a chosen one that was able to contact the dead?

Even if I had the opportunity to explain all of my WHAT IFs, would they be rejected or accepted by the people that attended the services?

I never had the opportunity to talk to Mannie again, nor did I feel it would serve a purpose.

Two days later, something occurred that gave me a lot to think about. You, too, may want to give it some serious thought.

I almost did not attend that Friday service at the Spiritualist Association, but a nagging urge to go kept me prompting me. Was it because I should make a private appointment with Rose Ann?

I dismissed that idea. Somehow having my fortune told never impressed me. Sure, I was curious. In fact, I had gone through several readings in the past, but I soon realized that the readers were just telling me what I wanted to hear or already knew.

I sense you are curious to know if I received or responded to a message while sitting in on the services. The answer is YES. For what it is worth, I'll tell you about it.

"We have a gentleman here today named Jack. He has a message for Kate," the medium said. There was no response. She again repeated she had a message for Kate. "Perhaps you know her as Katherine," she now suggested.

"My mother's name is Katherine," I volunteered.

"Yes, yes, this is the message you are to give her. Tell her Jack is waiting for her on the other side. She feels his presence but is confused. Jack does not mean to frighten her, only to assure her that he is protecting her."

That was the end of the message from the medium and the beginning of the questions for me.

Did my mother have a secret love affair with a guy named Jack? My dad's name is George, and he died twenty years ago. My mother was in her late sixties. Her only interest was cooking and going to church. Should I ask my mother about Jack the next time I call her?

I don't think so! I dropped the incident. It was too far-fetched. Besides, when I told my mother about my interest in the paranormal and that I was giving lectures on the subject, her response was, "Do you mean people actually pay to hear that stuff?"

"When you come home for vacation this summer, don't tell people what you are doing. They will think you are crazy," she spoke with quiet and desperate firmness.

WHAT IF she was right?

Let's get back to that memorable Friday. My intention was just to sit in the tea room and eavesdrop. That is until I walked through the door and saw a young woman sitting beside the heat register near the back hall, her eyes intently scanning a tourist's guide.

When I slid into the seat beside her, she looked up and took the opportunity to ask, "Oh, are you also a tourist? What brings you to this place?"

She put down her book and answered, "It was a friend at work that suggested it. She planned on being on this trip, but at the last minute, her son got sick." She then explained that she had a free afternoon, and the tour group she was with was flying to Paris in the morning.

"I live in New York, and I'm a proofreader for a fashion magazine." She told me her name was Andrea. She missed being plain only by the brilliant green of her eyes, which were magnified by the large circular glasses she wore a third of the way down her small nose. Her hair, a nondescript brown, was cut in ragged bangs across her forehead and hung helter-skelter to her shoulders, bordering her face like a bird's nest. The big round glasses gave the impression of an owl staring out at the world.

"Are you going to have a private session or go to a service?" I asked.

"My private session will be at 4:00 p.m. I had no place else to go, so I thought I would read here. I've never been to a service. Are you going?"

"I've been here all week and found it most interesting. If you care to go, I'll go with you. I'd like to hear what you think about all of this."

We got our tickets and headed upstairs. After getting seated, the medium came in, glanced uneasily over her shoulder, and took her place in front of the semicircle. Her thin fingers tensed in her lap; she began.

"We have a message for Andrea."

Andrea stood up, surprised, and stammered in bewilderment, "Are you talking to me?"

"Your Aunt M is here. She tells me your mother is with her. You are not to worry. Your aunt is taking care of her."

"But my Aunt Myrtle is dead, and my mother is alive," she whispered to me, and she sat down. The medium paused briefly and then added, "That is the end of the message." She then called another name.

The next moment Andrea got up, turned to me, and said, "I've got to get out of here." I followed her.

"How did the medium know I called my Aunt Myrtle, Aunt M? Was she trying to tell me that my mother is dead?" She gasped, not wanting to believe what she just heard.

"Let's go downstairs and call your mother," I suggested. "There was a telephone in the hall by the restrooms."

Andrea told me that she left her mother two days ago and she was fine. She said they both had their apartments in the same building. Her mother and her Aunt Myrtle lived together after her dad died. Aunt Myrtle died eight months ago, and her mother did not want to move in with her.

"Mother is only seventy-five. She plays bridge every Tuesday and never misses church on Sunday. She is fine; she is fine," she repeated as if trying to convince herself.

"Call her," I again suggested. She did. There was no response.

"She is probably out shopping."

"Does the building supervisor have a key to her apartment?"

"Why, yes. Mother and his wife are in the same bridge club."

"Call her. Tell her to go to your mother's apartment. If there's no answer, tell her to open the door with the key and check to see if your mother is all right. Give her the number and tell her to call you here and that you will be waiting to hear."

"That's a good idea," she said. She went back to call the supervisor's wife.

"We can hear the phone from here," I said as she returned. "Let me get us some tea while we wait," I suggested.

It was less than fifteen minutes when the ringing of the telephone summoned Andrea to hear something she was not ready to listen to. I heard the one-way conversation and her long pauses, reluctant to hang up, reluctant to lose that link. She wanted to have answers about the two days since she left home. She said she had called her mother last night, and she sounded fine.

"Yes, yes, I'll get the next plane home," she sighed before hanging up.

"I'll have to go back to my hotel and do some phoning and make arrangements. Why did this happen while I was here?" she questioned.

"It will be all right. Your aunt is with her, so that is really a blessing, knowing she has someone with her."

Later that day, when I got back to the hotel, I told my husband what happened, and he said, "Don't you think it is strange that she was there to get that message? It sounds to me like someone was directing her to go to that place."

"Perhaps."

As I mentioned at the beginning of this experience, you would be hearing my interpretation of how I sum up mediums. I'm sure you all have your opinions. If what you believe works for you, then, by all means, stay with it.

ARE YOU STILL IN BONDAGE?

DISCARDING OLD MINDSETS

At one time, I was fascinated with the crystal ball, and of course, I had to have one.

In my search for answers, I found it had credibility. Today, I have no need for crystal gazing. I find a person's eyes are the mirror to the soul.

But I will share my crystal-gazing experience with you later, in the *A Search for Answers* chapter.

"I need some answers," Brenda sobbed the morning she called. "Gary walked out on me. He just left a note saying he didn't want to be married to me any longer."

"How can I help?" I asked, wondering why she called me. I met Gary and Brenda at a Sunday evening metaphysical meeting. We occasionally chatted during the coffee break. She told me that she and Gary were yoga instructors, and they had recently moved to the Metroplex area.

"I heard that you read the crystal ball, and I want to know if you can see the reason why Gary left so abruptly. Is there another woman?" Her voice was fragile and shaking when she asked.

Instead of explaining that I was new at crystal ball gazing, my thoughts scampered vaguely around, and I heard myself inviting her to come right over. After she arrived, she told me that she had just been to the local psychic and that there was nothing the psychic could tell her.

All I do is ask the question as I gaze into the ball and wait for a picture answer to appear. "I never know what to expect," I told her as

111

we sat at the table. I encouraged her that she, too, should look at the ball. She declined my suggestion.

In a few minutes, I saw the word BONDAGE.

It seemed to be blinking like a neon sign, beckoning to get my attention. I then mentally asked a question, "What does bondage have to do with why Gary left?" The answer received telepathically was, *Thomas has your answer.*

"Do you know anyone by the name of Thomas?" I asked Brenda. The name meant nothing to me. "I'm sorry, but that's all I am seeing," I told her after about fifteen minutes of waiting for something more to happen.

"I can't understand what bondage means, and I don't know anyone named Thomas," she answered, her voice rough with anxiety.

"I have a friend that is very psychic, and sometimes we work together, sort of like a research project. She's coming over this afternoon to return some books, and maybe we can come up with some more information. I'll call you tonight if anything turns up," I volunteered. Her despair seemed to lessen as she left.

When my dear friend Angela arrived, I explained what happened earlier, and she was willing to help. After we sat with our eyes closed for about ten minutes, Angela suddenly announced, "I wanted you to go to Mass with me today. I just know we will get our answer for Brenda in church."

Since my crusade for self-awareness surfaced, I began to have a new outlook on life. The only way to describe it is that I began discarding all my old mindsets. Don't get me wrong. I would never discourage anyone from attending church. But for me at that time, it was not as important as it had been in the past.

The day Angela came over, it happened to be a Holy Day of Obligation, which meant good strong Catholics are obligated to attend mass on that day. At the time, I lived in Texas, and the Catholic University was only two blocks from my home. I knew that there was a Chapel on the grounds and probably would have a service.

Angela insisted that I call to get the details regarding their service. I was told Mass would be at three that afternoon.

"We must go," she insisted.

My attitude was, *What the heck! If this pleases her, I'll go.*

As we sat in the pew, surrounded by students waiting for the Mass to begin, a young priest came out of the vestibule. He stood for a moment, looking around at the congregation announced, "I'm Father Thomas, and I'm new on the campus. It is my understanding that at this Mass, there will be no sermon, but I feel compelled to discuss the subject of BONDAGE today." As he emphasized the word 'bondage,' his eyes locked on me as his head began nodding up and down as if acknowledging someone's instructions.

I gave a surprised gasp as I felt Angela nudge me on the arm. When I turned to look at her, she too nodded her head and grinned. I knew what she was thinking; *See, I told you that you can get answers by going to church.*

Father Thomas began explaining what the word bondage meant. As I listened, it started to make sense. He talked about the Israelites following Moses in the desert for forty years. He wasn't mocking their actions; he was trying to explain that in order to grow spiritually, one has to break loose from becoming too dependent on others to make decisions for you. "We need to learn to be independent and to be responsible for ourselves," he emphasized.

Perhaps Gary left Brenda so she could learn to be self-reliant. My observation of her, during the brief encounters we had, led me to believe she worshipped Gary. She hung on to his every word and constantly relied on his opinion about everything that was discussed at the meeting.

That evening I called Brenda to explain what happened and what bondage could infer. "It could well be referring to the relationship you and Gary had. Maybe he wasn't even aware of it... maybe he left so that you could grow spiritually and take on responsibility, so you could fend for yourself."

"To rely on someone is OK, but if you turn over all decisions and depend on a person too much, it can become unhealthy," I tried to choose my words carefully. She pretended she didn't understand and ended the conversation. That was the last time I heard from her period. I later learned she moved back to Ohio to be with her sister.

My story does not end here. Let me take you back to the chapel and explain what happened after Mass ended and we were leaving. Father Thomas was standing by the door greeting the departing students and shaking hands with them. As Angela and I approached him, he studied me intently, his eyes clouded with visions of the past, and he said, "Don't I know you? You look so familiar." I had the same feeling, but I drew a blank and answered, "Perhaps I remind you of someone. That happens every so often," I commented as I moved on.

For some reason, I wanted to explore this further. I felt so strongly that we have our answers if we are persistent in asking ourselves.

That evening, as I was sharing the day's activities with my husband, he became interested, encouraged me to 'run it into the ground' until I got an explanation. I'm a gal that does not believe in accidents, happenstances, or coincidences.

After I went to bed that night, I used the Silva Method technique that is always successful for me. I program myself to have a dream, to remember my dream, and to understand that dream. "I want to know if I knew Father Thomas before and where?" is the question I asked myself.

I awoke with the answer sometime in the middle of the night. I always have a pad and a pen on the nightstand. Sometimes I turn on the light and sit up in bed to write my dream; sometimes, I write keywords, which trigger the scenario so I can recall and write it down in the morning. That night I got out of bed, and I began to write.

You met in Spain. You were a nun; he was a monk. You taught religion to the village children. He tended to gardens, raising vegetables for the brothers at the nearby monastery. When the two of you met in the village, there was such a strong attraction, you both agreed to meet and get better acquainted. You would meet in the orchard, on the monastery grounds. To make a long story short, the two of you began 'monking' around. One day the Monsignor caught the two of you in the orchard and went ballistic. He informed the Mother Superior in the convent where you lived during that lifetime of your misconduct. You were punished for the rest of your life, scrubbing floors and assigned to tasks that were degrading.

I figured this must have been one of my bondage lifetimes.

Father Thomas, during that lifetime, was known as Brother Thomas, and was reprimanded by being sent to a far-off monastery, never to be seen or heard from again for committing sins of the flesh.

Funny thing… while I was getting this explanation, I felt that I was in Spain again, reliving the experience. I could even see the fat Monsignor with his disapproving frown and his cold, fierce eyes that reminded me of a falcon.

After I wrote down my impressions, I went back to bed. The last thought I had before falling asleep was, *my husband is going to get a laugh out of this when I tell him at breakfast.*

But my story still doesn't end there. You don't actually think I would drop the ball. The saying, 'gone but not forgotten,' is what prompted me to return to the Chapel several days later. I was hoping that I might run into Father Thomas not to take up where he left off so many years ago, but to see if, by chance, he also had some recognition, after all, when in the priesthood you do a lot of meditating. Who knows, I may have even told him of my dream? But alas, it was not meant to be.

As I was walking down the steps towards his chapel that morning, a heavyset man in priest robes confronted me. He stopped me and asked me what I was doing on campus. I told him I wanted to meditate in the chapel and that I found it a peaceful place. He stood a moment studying me, and all at once, his face twisted in anger as he began to lash out at me, "This campus and chapel are for students. Go back to your own parish. If I allowed anyone to come and go as they please, there would be no room for the students." I was so stunned by his outburst, I turned around, got my car, and left.

Of course, I relayed the details to my husband when he came home from work that evening. His only comment was, "Do you think he, too, recognized you? He may not have even known why he was so forceful. Now, what do you plan on doing?"

"I'll put that on the back burner to simmer, but now my curiosity is aroused, so you know I won't drop it," I replied.

I had to postpone further action because I went on a lecture tour for two weeks. Upon my return, ask my husband what he thought about me inviting Father Thomas over to dinner. "That should prove interesting," was the only comment he made.

I called the university the next morning and asked if I could speak to Father Thomas. The secretary that answered the phone informed me that Father Thomas was assigned to another campus, and she was instructed not to give out his address.

I only hope that I was not responsible for getting him sent to Siberia or some such remote place.

Believe me, when I say you don't need a crystal ball to see the future or to get answers. I'll have to admit it was fascinating and entertaining at the time.

I also experimented with Tarot cards, Astrology, and Numerology, to name a few. All have a certain amount of credibility. But when it comes down to the final analysis, our 'truth center,' which I believe is the soul urge, recognizes it as one of the experiences we had while in a physical body.

When I get answers from another dimension or from a spirit being or HEY!, it may be a vivid imagination; I use my vocabulary and expressions. If I get a cold chill running down my back, I accept it as *truth*. Does this sound familiar to any of you?

DR. JOSEPH MURPHY

BEACON OF INSPIRATION

I counted twenty-two egrets perched on the roof of the dormitory as I looked out the window this morning. I'm munching on a bran muffin and banana with my tea to start the day.

My neighbors next door who live on five acres have the uninvited pests/guests most of the summer. On every tree, you see hundreds of the snow-white herons, the bird that grows the long plumes hat makers or milliners call 'aigrettes.'

At one time, plume hunters used to kill so many egrets that there was a danger that none would be left. Since plume hats are no longer in style, they were left alone to continue breeding. Their number is increasing to a nuisance. They travel in large flocks, find a densely wooded area beside a lake, and take over. They are slowly taking over every green tree in the radius. My acres have mostly hedges, but they do fly all over the surrounding areas to broaden their territory.

Now, why did I have to give you a sermon on egrets this morning? I seem to focus a lot on birds. I'd better squelch that topic for fear of being accused of being a 'bird brain.'

What I feel led to share with you this morning is my encounter with another one of my interesting friends.

When I answered the telephone shortly before noon that day, little did I realize who would be sitting at my dinner table that evening.

"I'm Joseph Murphy. I've been invited to Dallas to give a lecture series. Norman Vincent Peale suggested I look you up. When is it convenient for us to meet?"

Without giving it a second thought? I suggested he come to dinner that evening. I'd never heard about Dr. Murphy's work, but the fact that he was a friend of Dr. Peale's prompted me to extend the invitation.

"Anything in particular you would like for dinner?" I asked. "Yes, a baked potato, ground round steak, peas, and carrots. I'll bring the scotch. And I want to talk to you privately," he added.

Dr. Murphy and his driver arrived promptly at seven with a bouquet of flowers. Five-foot, two inches tall, his eyes reminded me of my wisteria bush, blue with a purplish cast. He was in his mid-seventies; his withered complexion displayed a road map of laugh lines. Gregarious and assertive and soon discovered he was also a 'take charge' person.

Immediately after dinner, he lit a cigar, announced my husband and the young man that drove him, "Watch TV or get acquainted. I want to spend some private time with Mrs. Hadsell."

Dr. Joseph Murphy, Ph.D., DD (1898 to 1981), was born in Ireland. He was a world-renowned authority on mysticism and mind dynamics. The author of more than thirty books, he remains a beacon of enlightenment and inspiration for legions of loyal followers.

"I'm curious how you will interpret one of my personal experiences. I've never written about it in any of my books, nor do I intend to. I know what the reaction of the majority of people would be if I told them," he explained. "I don't wish to be accused of being a warlock or that I have the power of the devil."

He then began telling me the following story.

He was raised in a strict Catholic family and immediately began his studies after graduating from high school to become a priest. All of the ten Murphy siblings became active in the church. His six brothers were priests, and his three sisters were nuns. He eventually migrated to the USA and was assigned to a parish in California. He had some ideas. He wanted to explore, but the Catholic diocese in his district did not approve, so he took a leave of absence.

His only income was from a local radio station. He wrote the 'Thought For The Day,' which were uplifting sayings that were used as a public service. After renting a room, he began exploring the ideas that met with disapproval from his superiors. His goal was to live in a comfortable home, to have a garden with a water fountain, a stockade fence for privacy, and to produce program tapes.

With such a small income, he said that he ate a lot of peanut butter, crackers, and canned soup that heated on a hot plate.

For five months, two weeks, and three days, he was a recluse, devoting all of his time composing uplifting phrases and visualizing his goal.

"I would picture myself walking up to the house and sitting in the backyard by a water fountain, relaxing. Each time I went into meditation, I kept adding things that I would like in my home; original artwork, oriental carpets, a library with books from floor-to-ceiling, and a circular staircase that would lead me upstairs to a massive bedroom overlooking the Hollywood Hills. And yes, a room upstairs that would be soundproof, stocked with recording equipment and plenty of tapes so I could make self-help tapes covering all subject matters."

One day and knock on the door brought him out of his reverie and turned out to be the answer to his programming that included everything that he had been visualizing since being on his own.

An attorney representing a client that recently died told him he was the sole heir of their estate. The attorney had contacted the radio station for Dr. Murphy's address, as he had no telephone.

While he began explaining how all this came about, I sat back, pinching my arm to assure myself I was awake.

"The woman and I had never met. She was not a member of any church. The attorney told me that she heard me on the radio. In fact, she had written down the messages that I had composed and read daily. (I went into the radio station once a week and taped them for later airing.) The messages made such an impression on her that she wanted me to continue my work in broadcasting and writing," he explained as he sat, chewing on his cigar.

"Are you ready to see what you just inherited? You are going to be quite surprised," the attorney said as he drove me toward the Hollywood Hills. All I could think about was, "Now I can make tapes that will benefit and uplift the listeners."

"I was in total shock. Not that my programming had come to fruition, but it took such a short time. EVERYTHING I had programmed for had manifested. I almost blew it after we entered the home, and I saw the circular stairs leading to the second floor and asked. 'Is there a soundproof room upstairs?'"

Intense astonishment touched the attorney's pale face. He asked, "Have you been here before? How did you know there's a recording studio upstairs?"

"That's been a desire I have had for some time, making tapes of positive affirmations. I've found the majority of people have to read or hear something over and over before it sinks in. Listening to tapes repeatedly will help change their mindsets," I explained.

"Not only did I inherit all of the material goods, there was a clause in the will that took care of the taxes and a monthly upkeep of the property," he chuckled with happy memories as he related his story.

"Now my question to you is... how would you interpret what happened? How did every one of my goals become realized?"

"You connected with each other via telepathy," I answered.

"The woman, while listening to your Thoughts for the Day on the radio, was impressed with the messages you gave. She was sitting in the midst of all her prized possessions and decided that YOU were the person that she wanted to give them to. As she sat admiring each item, she was sending out a picture and thinking about you. You, in turn, were meditating and receiving her projections—thinking it was YOUR idea. You connected mentally. That's why, when you saw the property, it was like a dream come true."

"I don't blame you for not wanting to share this experience with the masses. They would still say that you were a witch or have help from the devil. A few might comprehend how it could happen, but why take chances?" I added.

"Are you being accused of using witchcraft since writing your experiences of winning a house, all the trips, cars, and merchandise?" He asked, turning his smile up a notch.

"I was anticipating the witchcraft accusations, so I deliberately coined the work WISHcraft in my book title, *The Name It & Claim It Game— WINeuvers for WISHcraft*. And, yes, to your question, I still get a lot of letters from excited people that read my book and tell me if their winnings by following my detailed steps. And what are you doing at the present time?" I asked.

"After I did some traveling and a lot of soul searching, I'm presently the Minister-Director of the Church of Divine Science in Los Angeles, and I still continue to do my daily radio programs. I also enjoy lecturing around the country. In the past few years, I've gone on a number of cruises," he answered.

Before Dr. Murphy left, he said he would send me copies of his books, which he did. I immediately noticed that he repeated many of the stories in the books verbatim. When we next made contact, I jokingly commented on the repetition of the antidotes. His comment was, "I figure if people hear or read something forty-two times, they will remember it."

The following are the names of some of the books he authored; *Amazing Laws of Cosmic Mind Power, The Power of Your Subconscious Mind*, and *The Miracle of Mind Dynamics*. (A number of his books are still available on the Internet.)

If there is a secret to achieving the desires of our heart, it must be, having a positive attitude. Refuse to admit failure and keep reminding yourself that there are no failures... only a delay in results. I realize that some goals are not accomplished as fast as you may want but hang in long enough and strong enough, and they will manifest. And the technique that has worked for me in the past and still works for me today is:

SELECT IT—PROJECT IT—EXPECT IT—COLLECT IT

LEVITATING

A NUISANCE

This is something I chose never to experience again. In fact, I really should keep it as a deep dark secret along with my desire to dance, but at this time, my philosophy again comes to mind:

LIFE GOES ON.
WHO CARES?
And, if some of you feel that I'm boasting, GET OVER IT!

Have you ever wanted to fly like Superman? Maybe just walk on water like Jesus? Would you be satisfied to levitate a little? Whatever your reason, mine was to show off to attract attention.

Yes, I've levitated, and it was not that uplifting. It proved to be a downright nuisance. Believe me; you will be better off leaving the levitating to Peter Pan and the Flying Nun.

The desire to levitate came to me shortly after taking a mental training class, the Silva Mind Control program. I began practicing techniques to use my mind more productively. It didn't take long before I began achieving phenomenal success in telepathy. Hunches became reality. Awareness was heightening. I became able to tell when people were mad, glad, or sad and to respond accordingly.

In my book *The Name It & Claim It Game,* I wrote about being positive in all areas. I shared my techniques with readers interested in using creative visualization and positive thinking to enter contests and sweepstakes. **Select It, Project It, Expect It,** and **Collect It** were my keys to success.

Soon I was receiving invitations from churches, colleges, and awareness centers around the country to give lectures and present workshops. That's when the idea to levitate first surfaced.

Why not? It could probably draw more people into my lectures on the Billy Graham service. I'd be able to show skeptics and non-believers

123

that everything is possible. Whatever the mind can conceive, it can achieve, I reasoned.

Training on a Trampoline

Jumping on my trampoline—willing myself to stay in mid-air became a daily ritual. My hopes were high, but that was all. I remained grounded.

"Maybe it's my weight," I thought. Perhaps I need to start a yoga class or meditate. It didn't take long to rule out yoga. The positions proved impossible, but I did meditate daily.

During this period of preparation, I read about Saint Thomas Aquinas, who, it is written, levitated. The 'Dumb Ox' (as some of his fellow students, in their ignorance, dubbed him) weighed over three hundred pounds. So it wasn't, I reasoned, the weight that kept me grounded.

One weekend a lecture engagement took me to Detroit. After the program, an elderly gentleman approached me; almost apologetically, he began talking.

"You don't really want to levitate, but I don't think you will believe me until it happens to you, so I'll tell you what you need to do. Pretend you are stroke swimming but hold your arms outstretched like this," he demonstrated.

My eyes widened in surprise as I wondered how he knew of my interest in levitation. Perceiving my unasked question, he responded, "I just had the feeling you were trying to levitate when I saw you on the TV talk show. Something told me to come and tell you about my levitating experiences."

He said that he lived in the country and how grateful he was for all the trees on his property because he could use them to hang on to when he began levitating. His only companion, a retriever, accompanied him on his daily walks through the woods.

"My dog would just stand and wait until I was able to balance myself. Such a nuisance... I wish it would stop," he said.

"I've never told anyone but you about my levitating. I know I would be considered a deranged character." He asked me not to mention our conversation to anyone. He did not dissuade me.

There is never any failure. Only a delay in results, I kept reminding myself. I continued practicing on my trampoline and doing daily meditations.

Several months after the Detroit incident, I woke up one morning feeling super. You won't catch me using the expression 'on top of the world' because these days, I'm extra careful what I think, say, or do. Feeling so charged, balanced, and grateful for all my blessings, I decided to attend the morning services at the chapel located on the grounds of the University of Dallas, a short distance from where I lived at the time.

After I left my car and walked fifty yards towards the chapel, something happened. Looking down at the ground, I realized it was below me—my body was floating, six inches in the air. The path to the chapel was downhill, and there were no trees or bushes nearby. I panicked.

Swimming in the Air

Then I remembered what the man told me in Detroit and began stroking in mid-air as though swimming. I balanced myself and began moving forward towards the chapel. Locking my mind on one of the pillars bordering the entrance, my plan was to wrap my arms around it and get back on the ground. I kept my eyes firmly on the goal and was soon able to accomplish this maneuver, although I was operating in a totally unfamiliar environment. As I hastily returned to solid ground once more, I felt tremendous relief. I kept clinging to the pillar until, with such a jerk, the voices of students arriving for services brought me back to reality and grounded me—literally.

"Thank God. No one saw me," I thought as I joined the students entering the chapel, heaving a sigh of relief. When the service was over, I waited until everyone left before I ventured outside.

There was no repeat performance! It hasn't happened since.

Floating in Her Sleep

I occasionally mentioned this incident, usually as a joke, to my students in my center in Alvarado, Texas, where I teach self-awareness classes. Several years ago, eight young ladies were attending a weekend workshop. One of the girls heard my lecture and encouraged her co-workers and friends to come to a weekend retreat.

Tired after a long journey, they decided to retire early in preparation for the next day's classes. One of the girls was still in the library when I left to go to my quarters. The next morning she was the first one in the center, and an adventurous toss of her head, she asked, "Do you know what I saw—or thought I saw—last night?"

I shook my head.

"Dana was floating in mid-air about a foot above her bed. My bed is beside hers. Talk about being surprised. I was so startled I froze for a moment. I was reluctant to wake her for fear she might fall. Everyone else was already asleep, so I just sat in my bed and watched. In about fifteen minutes, she floated back down and turned over. She never did wake up."

Before I could reply, Dana and several other girls walked into the center.

"Dana, you sure did scare me last night floating over your bed. I was afraid you might hurt yourself if I woke you."

Dana blushed, her misery evident. "I was hoping I wouldn't do that anymore… " she whispered.

"What are you talking about? Tell us," the girls clamored. There would be no peace until Dana explained the mystery.

She told us that as a child, she had seen her mother float in mid-air on numerous occasions. Sometimes while she was napping on the couch, her mother's body would rise several inches.

"When I was about six years old, my mother had just given birth to her seventh child at home. She had a difficult time. Grandmother came to take care of us. She cautioned us not to go into mother's room because she needed a rest," she explained.

"One evening, open the door to look in her room. The rest of the family was watching TV. I saw Mother floating towards the ceiling. I was so frightened. I ran to call my dad. He and Grandmother ran into her room. Dad got on the bed and pulled mother back down as we watched," she bent her head and studied her hands to compose herself before continuing.

"After dad calmed down, he explained that the devil was trying to take our mother from us. 'She is a good mother, and if we all pray, the devil cannot take her,'" he assured us.

"Grandmother was already on her knees, kissing the rosary she always carried in her pocket. From that night on, before going to bed until Mother was up and well, we recited the rosary. Dad and Grandmother told us to never tell anyone. We listened and promised we would tell no one."

"People just won't understand, they told us. I have never told this to anyone before now," she continued.

"When I was eight years old, I got chicken pox and was running a high fever. I remember it was shortly before Thanksgiving. I guess my dad and mother thought I was sleeping, but I heard Mother say, 'Yes, I'll tell her when she gets better.'"

"Several days later, Mother told me that I floated like she did, but not to worry. The angels would take care of me because I was a good girl. She also said I was the only child of hers that floated in that would be our secret."

Family Kept Her Safe

"I had so much confidence and admiration for my parents and grandmother that I never felt frightened. I believed what they told me, and I felt they would protect and keep me safe."

"Sometimes, over the years (after I left home and had my own apartment), I would recall these experiences when I was watching a far-out movie or my favorite television program, Star Trek. I would immediately put it out of my mind because I thought that it might start up again if I dwelled on it."

Everyone sat spellbound as Dana told her story. Several of the girls seemed uncomfortable, so I decided it was an appropriate time to share my own levitation experience.

"Some people spend thousands of dollars taking courses to learn how to levitate," I told them.

Why it happened to Dana and her mother, I can only theorize. Perhaps in another lifetime, they mastered yoga. Perhaps they became so detached from the body that they learned to rise above it. "I'm certainly no expert on the subject," I explained. "I'm certain about one thing; the Devil is not out to get you if you have this gift."

As Dana listened, her face began to relax. Squaring her shoulders, she sighed as if releasing a burden. Perhaps she was practicing a new kind of levitation. By removing the dead weight of false beliefs imposed in childhood by well-meaning but misinformed parents, her spirit was literally rising before our eyes.

That evening there was no levitation and very little sleep. The girls stayed awake to see if Dana would 'float' again, but alas, they were disappointed.

"It is important that you respect Dana and honor her by being silent about the events that occurred during this retreat. This is her request and decision," I informed the students before their departure.

It has been several years since I last saw Dana. Earlier this year, I received an unexpected call from her. She met a young man, and they are to be married in the near future. Her father passed on, and her mother remarried. Since the weekend at the Center, she read about levitation, and "I understand as much as I care to," she told me.

There has been no further levitation to her knowledge. Before saying goodbye, we laughed together and agreed we would be happy to remain grounded—at least in this lifetime.

If levitation is your interest, I suggest you reread my experience. The desire is the criteria for many of our manifestations.

Strange thing... when something you desire is accomplished, ask yourself... was this really worth the time and effort? My answer today is: I'll leave the levitating to Superman or Mary Poppins.

HELP IS JUST A THOUGHT AWAY

I don't like to dredge up SAD memories, but that's reality. It's the GLAD, SAD, and MAD of life.

In the morning paper, the front page carried a story about two local teenage boys dying in an automobile accident over the weekend.

Perhaps my experience can help someone understand that help is just a thought away, even if we can't see in other dimensions. Here is my story that took place in May of 1954.

"He was wild-eyed, sobbing, grabbing at me and pleading for me to help him. I could feel his grip on my arm. As I tried to calm him down." My 17-year-old son, Chris, was describing a nightmare he just had about his best friend, Jeff.

"What do you make of it?" he asked, his voice filled with concern as he stood in front of me, visibly shaken.

It was Monday morning. My husband had already left for work, and I was having my second cup of coffee when Chris burst into the kitchen. "I know it was just a dream, but it seemed so real. What do you make of it?" he again asked as he began buttering a bran muffin and waiting for an answer. He had to be at school 30 minutes early today. It was his senior year, and all the seniors were to meet in the auditorium to rehearse for graduation exercises that would take place on Friday.

"It could mean any number of things," I began explaining, "A TV show or movie you recently watched and used Jeff to recreate the emotional events. You guys are such close buddies. Maybe Jeff was watching a movie and thinking about you, wishing you were with them so you could watch it together. Another possibility would be precognitive—meaning something happened to Jeff, and he was trying to reach you telepathically," I offered as an explanation. "When you see Jeff today, ask him if he thought about you while he was watching a scary movie," I suggested.

Jeff and my son spent most of their after-school hours in the garage working on Chris' Corvette. Beyond his ability to follow car manual instructions well, Jeff was simply a good mechanic. He helped his father, who was the owner of the used car dealership in town. By the age of ten, he spent most of his time at his dad's garage watching the mechanics whose job it was to get the trade-ins to run in top condition. Last year his parents divorced. His dad moved to Houston and opened a dealership there. His mother remarried. Jeff was having difficulty adjusting to his stepdad. He was at our place most of the time. I kidded him and said that I was ready to adopt him.

This was the weekend Chris planned on going to Houston with Jeff to help him pick out a car. Jeff's dad sent airline tickets for the two boys to fly down. As a graduation gift, he told Jeff he could pick out any car on the lot. He and Chris would drive the car back home. That's all the boys talked about. Chris had had his bags packed that Friday morning. They would catch a plane after school. But there was a change of plans. Chris and Jeff worked at the freight docks on weekends when freight was backlogged. The pay was good, and they considered themselves lucky to have the opportunity to supplement their income. It took a lot of money to keep Chris' temperamental car running.

That afternoon, while Chris was in school, his boss called. When he returned the call, he was elated. Chris was given the opportunity to work Friday, Saturday, and Sunday. He would be paid double time on Sunday. This meant he could buy new tires and paint his car. The offer was too good to turn down. He called Jeff and asked if they could go to Houston the following weekend. Jeff was disappointed, but when he heard how much money Chris would be making, he said, "Go for it. I'll ask Mark to go with me." Mark was also a good friend of the two boys, and he was delighted when Jeff invited him to go in Chris' place. The last words Jeff said to Chris were, "I'm bringing home a Corvette. My dad said he had three of them on the lot, and I could have one of them."

I was just getting ready to gather the laundry when the phone rang. It was Jeff's aunt. She was trying to reach Chris to ask him to be a pallbearer for Jeff's funeral.

I gasped when I heard what she said. "This can't be true."

"I'm sorry, I assumed you knew that Jeff was killed in an automobile accident on his way home from Houston," she explained.

"What happened to Mark?" I asked.

"He is in a coma and is not expected to live," she replied. I told her that my husband and I spent the weekend at her lake cabin, and Chris worked all weekend, so if anyone called, we were not available.

That afternoon when Chris got in from school. He was pale and shaken. He told me about driving into the school parking lot, and as he was walking toward the school, he met two of his classmates. They asked him why he hadn't gone to Houston with Jeff. He told them that he had to work, and Mark went instead. "I asked if they saw Jeff's car and if he got a Corvette."

"You mean you don't know Jeff was killed and Mark is in critical condition?" one of the boys asked him.

At first, Chris thought it was a cruel joke. "I questioned why anybody would want to pull a dumb stunt like that, but they were too serious," he explained.

"I wanted to laugh… Jeff being gone was absurd! I wanted to cry… instead; I just made an excuse and told them I left a notebook in the car and I would meet up with them later. I had to get away from them, off to myself for only a minute. The lump in my throat was choking me. When I got to the car and slid behind the wheel, I began shaking. It felt like I'd be sick to my stomach." Tragedy had etched composure and dignity into his face as he stood there, relating his feelings.

"This is understandable. This is the first time in your seventeen years that you have experienced personal grief. I was there when my father died. I felt like I was being torn apart." I hope my story would console him.

"When I got to the gym, the principal was making the announcement about Jeff and Mark's accident. He said the funeral was to be on Wednesday afternoon, and the senior class would be excused to attend the service. Tammy, Jeff's girlfriend, came running over to me and asked why I hadn't gone to Houston with Jeff. In fact, everyone was curious to know," he muttered uneasily.

"Jeff was in study hall with me this afternoon. It felt like he was pulling on my shirt yelling, 'Chris, tell them that I'm not dead.' Maybe it was just a dream. I kept dozing off from lack of sleep," he said, searching for a plausible explanation. His sense of loss was beyond tears.

"Let's go to the den and get quiet. Perhaps we can help him," I suggested.

It couldn't have been but a few moments before Jeff appeared. He stood right in front of us. His eyes gleamed like glassy volcanic rock and were filled with tears of frustration.

"Mrs. Hadsell, help me. Tell my parents that I'm not dead. They can't see me; they won't listen to me. My mother blames my dad for giving me a car. My dad just sits in a chair crying."

Jeff was telepathically communicating with me. I could see him and understood what he was thinking. My son is an excellent receiver. He always has and is still able to pick up my telepathic messages. However, he is not able to see in the other dimensions.

I began explaining to Jeff that the automobile accident damaged his body beyond repair, but he was not buying it. He stood before us, ranting and raving. "I'm not dead, I'm not dead," he repeated over and over.

"Someone, please help me," I pleaded. It couldn't have been more than ten seconds before a tall thin gentleman appeared and stood beside Jeff. He put his hand on Jeff's shoulder. When Jeff became aware of his presence, he turned to look at him and said, "Grandpa, what are you doing here? Your dead," he stammered in bewilderment.

"Come with me," the old man said, nodding as he led Jeff to a light that was behind them. The next moment the entire scene faded as I gave a sigh of relief.

Does this sound like it may be an episode from a TV show, the GHOST WHISPERER? It does to me, as I recall the incident.

Helping people crossover into the light into 'another dimension' is not my job, nor my responsibility. Be assured when it's time to leave your worn-out body; you will have help and be welcomed by family and friends.

I did not feel the need to tell Jeff's parents what Chris and I experienced that day. Sometimes it's best to let things be. We all have learning experiences. We all set up our GLAD, SAD, and MAD periods. Do we learn from them? If not, as the saying goes... history will repeat itself!

PERU ASSIGNMENT

LOOK FOR THREE SIGNS
BEFORE TAKING ACTION

If you have gotten this far reading my book, then you must be aware that for me, LIFE IS ONE DARN THING AFTER ANOTHER. You can't say that I haven't had my share of off-the-wall experiences, but this assignment kept me on my toes all the while I was in South America.

I think of Peru every time I eat a mango because I had two for breakfast every morning the entire time I was there.

Now I will share with you what took me to Peru. It was just another assignment I really was not too keen about. But I had a choice.

The Assignment

I was in the bedroom when suddenly, I had the feeling that someone was watching me. I looked up to see a young man standing in the middle of the room, looking at me with penetrating dark eyes. I tried yelling out but momentarily was so paralyzed with fear that no sound came.

This happens occasionally. When one experiences a nightmare in the Dream State. Except I was wide awake.

The only sound that morning came from the patio where the birds were chirping their gratitude for the seeds we put in their feeder box.

I locked the door at the Center after I arrived and left the blinds closed. I got up that early that morning to prepare for three students who were coming from Houston to take awareness classes. They would be arriving about 4:00 p.m. I was sitting in my comfortable chair, sipping on my second cup of tea, writing out menus. Our living quarters were conveniently located across the patio from the Center.

I am certain the young man standing in the middle of the room could sense my fear because he started to smile, making me feel more at ease. Before I could utter a word, he began mentally communicating, "You are to be in Peru before the 16th of November. It is imperative for you to be there. You are to save a friend from engaging in a foolish venture. I will be there to help you."

The next moment he was gone.

Determined not to fall victim to the panic that hovered just below the surface, I jotted down the date when I received the message 8:15 a.m. on November 8th. I also wrote a description of the visitor: tall, slender, a commanding manner, serious. I had the impression that his message was more like a plea than a request.

When I was still feeling as if my heart was going to come right through my chest, the sound of the front door opening brought me back to the NOW. I watched my husband enter and let out a sigh of relief. No matter how many times I've had the experience of seeing into the fourth dimension, I still get unglued whenever it happens.

"You're up early," he greeted. There was something about the sound of his voice, something about that quiet, reassuring tone that instantly eased my anxiety.

"Am I glad to see you. You just missed meeting my uninvited guest," I said as I began relating what had just taken place. "What do you think that was all about?"

"If it has any significance, you should be getting two more signs. Don't you teach your students that they should always wait for three signs before taking action?" he reminded me.

"You are right. If this is an assignment, then the other two signs had better come fast. I still have plans to leave for Sedona, Arizona, on November 28th."

Earlier in June of that year, I had the opportunity to spend three days in Sedona. There was so much going on I decided to go back and spend at least a month investigating psychics and the many people that seem to gravitate to that special place to channel. While there, I met a woman at one of the meetings. I told her of my plans to return in the fall.

"You're just the person I'm looking for to house sit. If you are available during the month of December, I'll let you use my place during your stay," she offered.

I was elated. We finalized our plans before I left. She told me that her plan was to spend the month with her sister in Hawaii. I would drive my car and be in Sedona by the 30th. She would leave on December 1st. Several of my friends would join me for a few days during the month. The last week my husband would fly down, and we would drive back home together. It was a done deal.

My husband wanted to know more about my visitor. After fixing himself a cup of coffee, he sat down so we could discuss it in more detail. He was aware that over the years, I'd had many fourth dimension visitations. Because they never identify themselves with a name, I refer to them as <u>messengers</u>.

Some appear in dreams to instruct or remind me that I have chosen to experiment in the physical vibration to be of service. Some request the temporary use of my body to communicate with souls in the physical realm that are in jeopardy, confused, or simply needing to be reminded that they are never alone—that somebody is always near to help.

I never am certain what the purpose is until it is accomplished. Nor do I have an answer as to what the outcome will be. A familiar phrase explains it thus: *nothing is ever cut and dried; free will still reigns.*

"Who do you know in Peru, and did this messenger ever appear to you before?" my husband asked.

"No, I did not recognize him, and the only person I know from Peru is a young man I met while I was a speaker at the International Mind Control convention two years ago. The young man was in Laredo, taking teacher training to become an instructor with the program. He said he was impressed by my research and wanted me to come to Peru to give self-awareness workshops."

All I knew about Peru was what I heard on the news. It did not sound inviting. Constant government unrest, curfews, and rioting in the streets were common occurrences. I had declined the invitation. I had plenty of places to lecture elsewhere, where language and physical safety would not be a hindrance.

During the rest of my stay at the convention, every time I met the young man, he became more persistent, asking me to reconsider. My answer remained a definite NO! I never heard from him after he returned home, so I assumed that it was a dead issue.

Now today, he came to mind. I certainly had not considered him a friend after our brief encounter. Yet, the messenger called him my friend.

Waiting for a Third Sign

It did not take long for the second sign to appear. In the morning mail, I received a note from the woman in Sedona telling me that plans for me to house sit had changed. She had to undergo surgery, and her sister was coming to care for her while she recuperated. My first reaction was disappointment. This meant I would have to get busy and arrange to find another place for my month's stay. I did not want to disappoint my friends that had rearranged their schedules to join me.

"Look at it this way," my husband pointed out when I told him about the letter. "This may be your second sign."

That evening, after my students arrived, we were sitting in the gazebo talking when the telephone rang.

"Mrs. Hadsell, this is David. We met two years ago in Laredo. Do you remember that I asked you to come to Peru at the time, and you declined? Well, I have an offer now you will not be able to refuse," the excitement in his voice was evident. He told me that he could not explain the project he and some friends had planned because someone might be listening in on the conversation. "We need you and want to include you. I will pay for all your expenses, and I will set up classes for you during your stay. You will be my houseguest as long as you are here, and I will send you to Cusco and Machu Picchu and… " His voice broke mid-sentence. "What else will it take for you to be here by the 16th of November?"

Too startled by his proposal to offer any objection, my sixth sense finally kicked in, and I felt my defenses weakening when I heard him mention the date, November 16th. The same date the messenger had given.

"Why is the 16th so important?" I asked.

"I'll fill you in after you arrive," is all he would tell me.

Intense astonishment surfaced when I realized I had just received the THIRD SIGN.

"I'll make travel arrangements in the morning. Call me tomorrow evening, and I'll have a definite date for my arrival."

I KNEW I had to go, that it was an assignment. A cold chill ran down my spine, which always seemed to occur to let me know what I had heard, seen, or read was TRUTH.

"Fools rush in where angels fear to tread" kept running through my head as I boarded PanAm to Miami on November 12th, 1986.

After a five-hour layover, Aeroperú was on the way to Peru. We had one stop in Ecuador for an hour and arrived in Peru at 9:00 a.m., November 13th. We went directly to David's home, a stone's throw from the Pacific Ocean.

Immediately, I felt at home in the five-level spacious mansion. Most of the exterior walls were glass panels that overlooked a well-kept flower garden. A twelve-foot high brick wall surrounding the property provided privacy and security. The maid, gardener, and painter kept the premises in picture-book condition. Because of the poverty in Peru, robbery is common. The affluent Peruvians have their homes surrounded by walls and have security guards walking their areas around the clock.

After unpacking and soaking in a hot bath, I laid down for a two-hour nap. We went out for pizza, and at 7:00 p.m., we were to meet with Rouel, the man who organized the plan for this adventure. He would clue me in as to why it was so important that I needed to be in Peru.

Promptly at 7:00 p.m., Rouel arrived. A short, chubby round-faced man, he was overly polite. He spoke some English but kept apologizing and looking at David, asking questions in Spanish. Rouel had organized a party of eleven men to go on a 'dig' (as he called it). He explained how he and a friend had discovered a cove on the shoreline of the ocean and decided to tie up their boat and look around. They discovered a cave and wanted to investigate further.

"The strangest thing happened," he explained. "When we stepped into the cave, there was a force that seemed to be pushing us out. We both got cold chills and were downright scared. We then noticed the pieces of slick wood on the sand." Rouel pulled out several pieces of wood from his briefcase. The wood looked like it may have been painted deep rust at one time. Rouel laid them on the table for me to examine. He said that he had taken the wood to be analyzed by museum experts and was told it was approximately three hundred years old.

He also explained how he went to a number of local psychics who told him it came from a ship that was on its way back to Spain. A storm at sea dashed the ship against the rocks during a return trip where the Spaniards were transporting bars of gold. There had been survivors, and they were able to retrieve a portion of the gold bars, which they stored in the cave. The sailors were in wait to be rescued, but it did not happen. The psychics told Rouel that the Spaniards are still guarding the gold, and that was the energy he and his friend felt.

Sound far-fetched? Hang in; the story is better.

Rouel returned to the site several days later and again attempted to enter the cave. This time, he swore he saw five or six men coming toward him. "I couldn't get to my boat fast enough to get out of there," he said.

"And how do you think I can help?" I asked.

"David told us he was impressed with your ability to see in the fourth dimension. He said that you could communicate with the spirits and convince them that we would use the gold for good. I figure if you tell them that we will donate a significant portion to the poor in Peru, they might let us have the gold," he answered.

For a moment, I looked at the two of them sitting at the table and got up. "Let me fix a pot of coffee, and we can run through this again," I said as I headed for the kitchen. I had something else in mind.

"Help! Help! I need some BIG TIME help explaining to David why this pie-in-the-sky plan is foolhardy," I pleaded softly.

"I'm here, and I'm ready to take over when we get back in there." It was a telepathic message from the same messenger that appeared to me in my center five days earlier. Not only was I relieved, but I was also interested in what would happen next.

Perhaps I should explain that I'm not a trance medium that becomes oblivious to what transpires. I'm fully conscious and am aware when the residence of my voice changes. When that happens, I know someone in the fourth dimension is using my vocal cords to convey a message. Many times, words are used that are not part of my vocabulary.

In just a few minutes, I join David and Rouel with the coffee. I was ready for anything after I saw the same messenger that appeared to me earlier, standing behind David.

In a moment, I began relating what I was telepathically receiving. "There is a small man with grey hair that talks a lot when he drinks? He's part of your group. Last week he was at a bar with friends and began boasting about how he was going to get rich. He told them he was going to go on a dig with a party that he knew where the bars of gold to be found."

"Why yes, I know you were talking about," Rouel said with a surprised look on his face. "I had a feeling that he couldn't be trusted, but he put up the initial money that we all chipped in for supplies."

The messenger continued using telepathy, telling me what to say. "Surely, you are aware that any relic or treasure discovered on Peruvian soil automatically belongs to your government. Because the present government is so corrupt and infiltrated with mercenaries, not only will your finds be confiscated, but your lives will be in jeopardy. I urge you to ABORT!." Turning to David, I continued and said, "David, there will be other opportunities less dangerous for you to benefit the poor. I'm aware of your kind heart, but this is not the way to obtain funds for your project."

"Why should we abort our plans? We are prepared and ready, and we will have weapons to defend ourselves," Rouel growled.

"Perhaps you are not aware that you are presently being watched by your government. I suggest you call a friend, tell him where you are. Ask him to park at the end of the street and wait until he sees your car leave. When you leave, do not go directly home; rather, take a circuitous route. Direct your friend to stay a comfortable distance from you. When you arrive home, wait for his call. He will confirm that you were followed. Next, call David so he can be convinced that this excursion is foolhardy."

As I was explaining this to David and Rouel, I saw a transformation on Rouel's face. His brown eyes grew hard, glittering, holding a wild look that reminded me of a wolf. One so trapped and desperate that it would gnaw off its own leg, if necessary, just to escape. I knew this man was cruel and evil, and I wanted nothing to do with his plan.

"I can hurt anybody that interferes with my plans, worse than they ever dreamed, lady," Rouel hissed.

For a long moment, I hardly dared breathe. This man was teetering on some kind of emotional edge, and I was not sure he even knew where he was.

Rouel closed his eyes and threw back his head. An instant later, in a brusque tone, said, "I better make that call and find out if I'm really being followed."

I was certain he was sensing my distrust of him but was trying to get a handle on his anger. After a few minutes, he came out of David's office and said he had better be going. "I'll wait in your foyer until my friend drives by and has time to circle, then follow me. I will call you later and let you know."

Before he left, he looked at me and asked, "How long are you going to be here? If we can't go on the 16th, I want to know when it'll be safe."

"I have no idea, but I feel you should drop this whole idea."

This was something that he did not want to hear, I sensed, as he left the room. Later that evening, he called David. "She was right. We have to postpone this until later, and I'll take care of that guy that caused this delay."

I now accepted the fact that my reason for being in Peru was to keep naïve David from embarking on this dig. To convince him that Rouel was an unsavory character and to sever further ties with him. Now I knew the message that kept running through my mind: *'Fools rush in where angels fear to tread'* was meant for David.

I am always grateful for all the help I received from the other realm, and each night before falling asleep, I thank my visible and invisible helpers.

When I awoke the following morning, I knew my assignment in Peru had just begun. It kept me there for the next two and a half months.

The next afternoon, David invited his friends over for coffee and to meet me. One of the guests, an artist from Prague, recognized me immediately.

As she stood in front of me, and her eyes got weepy as she embraced me. "Oh, Sister, it is so good to see you again."

It took me a moment to connect before I remembered that we were together, in a past life, in Spain in a convent of Catholic nuns teaching children. I learned she spoke seven languages and married a Peruvian.

"You are going to be here a long time," she said. "While you are here, I will be your translator."

For some reason, when I did my packing to come to Peru, I stuck in my Tarot cards as an afterthought, never dreaming that I would be using them on a daily basis. I personally feel that one can read people without the use of cards, but as my friend explained, "People are fascinated by anyone that reads the cards—use them."

For the next month, I read the cards for doctors, lawyers, merchants, and thieves. Most of the affluent Peruvian could speak English. For the others that could not, my friend sat beside me as my interpreter. She became my secretary as well as my dear friend.

There were hundreds of people that came for readings. Each one of them had a problem and was looking for a solution. Most of the time, the clients brought their guidance with them. My friend could also see in the fourth dimension, and we work closely together. I am certain we were used as channels to help people help themselves.

Many times, I would write out an affirmation for them to repeat to eliminate a negative behavior pattern that kept them from progressing spiritually. When someone came with the physical challenge that the doctors were not able to help, I would explain to them about energy, emotions, and our thinking.

One of my favorite affirmations, one I shared with you earlier, and I feel bears repeating, is by Frank Outlaw:

Watch your thoughts, they become words;
Watch your words, they become actions;
Watch your actions, they become habits;
Watch your habits, they become character,
Watch your character, for it becomes your destiny.

I also wrote out affirmations according to their needs. For example:

In the past, I had this problem… a bad relationship… a physical
problem… etc.
I refuse to live in the past.
I will no longer give it energy.
I am healed.

Another affirmation that I borrowed from the book *Thinking and Destiny* by Harold Percival:

Every atom in my body thrill with life to keep me well.
Every molecule within me carries health from cell to cell.
Cells and organs in all systems
Build for lasting strength and youth.
Work in harmony by the conscious light of truth.
To rejuvenate, recharge and reenergize this body.

Illusion

I also taught self-awareness classes and investigated the local healers. A student told me about a local healer known as the 'Egg Lady' by the natives. The student was so impressed by her healing that she shared her personal experience.

144

"When I have a physical problem, I called the Egg Lady. All I have to do is bring a fresh dozen eggs," she told me. "I lay on a cot in her office, and we pray together while she passes the egg over my body. In a minute or so, she cracks open the egg and pours it into a small bowl on the table, and asks me to look at it. Sometimes it is full of blood, sometimes it's slimy black or brown, and often as a foul odor. She pours the egg into the bucket and repeats the healing until the egg is clean. She can pull up all the germs, infection, foreign growth, or even a hex that someone puts on me. I just pay her what I can afford," she explained.

"Oh, I'd like to meet her," I exclaimed with genuine interest.

David called and made an appointment for me. When I got there with my dozen eggs, I was led into her small office. After getting comfortable on a cot, I waited for her to begin the healing.

Instead, she said, "I can't heal you. You know what I am doing. I can only heal people that have faith and believe that the foreign object I mentally project into the eggs come out of their body." She studied me a moment, waiting for a response.

I sat up, and we began talking. "I'm not here to discredit you. I was told about you by one of the women you healed, and I wanted to meet you. You must be an excellent 'suggestologist' and illusionist. I'm curious to find out how you got started as a healer," I asked, using my non-intrusive approach.

We had a nice chat. She told me her mother and grandmother had also healed with eggs and that many people were healed because of their faith. In this society, she explained, this was her only means of making a living. She also said that on occasion, she would tell people to go elsewhere—that she was not able to heal them.

I sensed the genuine concern she had to help people, and I sincerely liked her.

Short Detour to MEXICO

One incident where 'suggestology' and illusion backfired was with one of the psychic surgeons that made a comfortable living with his mental powers.

A friend and I joined a group of fifteen people that went to Mazatlán, Mexico, to spend five days with a 'psychic surgeon.' Unfortunately, this psychic surgeon was in the greed and power mode and indirectly caused the death of one of the men in our group.

When first meeting the so-called psychic surgeon, he came across as being a bit too cocky and confident. He introduced his brother and cousin as helpers the first evening at the orientation meeting. We were asked to sign up for appointments for the following time he was available.

In our group, there was a man who had a pacemaker. He firmly believed that if he had a healing and had his pacemaker removed, he could function without it. His wife later told us that he requested the psychic surgeon remove the pacemaker.

"When he got back to our room after the surgery, he was on cloud nine—telling me he no longer needed the pacemaker. He told me he saw the pacemaker in the surgeon's hands after the surgeon removed it. He said he felt like his old self," his wife explained.

"The next morning, he got up bed started doing push-ups for about fifteen minutes. I was concerned that he was overdoing it and asked him to stop several times, but he continued. All of a sudden, he collapsed. I summoned help, but before the paramedics arrived, he was dead," she carefully related.

When the psychic surgeon heard what happened, he packed up and left immediately. Yes, there are still many people that are naive and gullible, and there are still charlatans and dishonest people.

It is the responsibility of each of us to use discernment.

Don't Steal, Don't Lie, Don't Be Lazy

I am a people watcher, and after I became familiar with the area where David lived, I would venture out on my own to the market. I noticed people chatting, and before they walked off, they would bow their heads and say, *"Ama sua. Ama llulla. Ama quella."* The other person would bow their head, nod, and say, *"Quampas jinallatag."*

Curious, I asked Davis what it was all about. He explained, "In the USA, before parting company, you usually end the conversation by saying, 'Have a nice day.' In Peru, the native parting is 'Don't steal. Don't lie. Don't be lazy.' the reply is, 'To you likewise.'"

The second week I was in Peru, I left for a five-day excursion to Cusco and Machu-Picchu. I had quite an adjustment with the altitude change. I get nose bleeds when I go to Denver, Colorado, where the altitude is a mere mile above sea level. In the Andes, it is two and a half miles high. The first two days, I had fierce headaches as well as nose bleeds. Fortunately, the hotels are prepared for newcomers. They have oxygen available, and guests are served cocoa tea (cocaine tea) after arriving, which helps them make the adjustment.

My personal guide during my stay in Cusco was a special person. As we stopped to view the ruins or tour the buildings, the urchins were everywhere. Their dirty little faces look up at you with their big black eyes, and they hold out their hands for money. The guide stopped at the bakery and market to buy rolls and oranges to pass out. "Never give up children money," he explained. "They take it home to their parents who use it for their drinking habit, and many times the children are left hungry."

When we arrived at the Sun Temple, I noticed a transformation take place with the guide. He became sad as he explained what took place after Spain invaded Peru and how the Spanish took over the temple, killing the priests and melted the gold into bars to be sent back to Spain. He also discussed how they handled the inquisition to remove the idol gods and replaced them with the Jesus, Mary, and Joseph story that they were now required to worship.

I got the feeling that he was one of the priests at the time and that he was mentally reliving that lifetime.

There were so many places in Peru that I was in total awe over. One of the most memorable places I found was in Cusco. It was a church with rows of altars. Some of the alters were made of gold. One was designed and built with two tons of silver. There were hand-carved wood altars that took years to complete. The church had four hundred wall paintings; each one was twelve feet by twenty-four feet with gold frames.

What an unbelievable display of talent.

As for Manchu Picchu, each person I talked to had their own story. During my stay, I was able to see through walls and read minds. Was it the altitude, the energy? All I know is, so many things happened to me; it was like everything was so clear I could see and hear forever.

I stayed in the hotel one night and was ready to leave the next day. There were so many fourth dimension beings communicating it was confusing and frustrating. That was one experience I have no intention of repeating.

Upon my return home, I had a lot to think about. As I mentioned earlier, I kept a daily journal, not only of my trip to Peru but all of the experiences I have shared with you.

I have learned to wait for three signs before venturing into anything of significance. I strongly urge you to do the same.

One of my best techniques for changing past mindsets is to repeat affirmations. I suggested that you make a tape and listen to it at night.

There are a number of people that have the power to mentally project their wishes so you can accommodate their needs. If you've ever seen a demonstration by a hypnotist, that should tell you what some people are capable of doing.

My advice is to DISCERN!

A SEARCH FOR ANSWERS

LESSONS FROM THE PAST ARE DOCUMENTED IN
THE AKASHIC HALL OF RECORDS

I behold that when a person dies,
His soul turns to earth,
Another mother gives him birth,
Arrayed in some new flesh disguise,
With sturdier limbs and brighter brain,
The old soul takes the road again.
John Masefield (1878- 1967)

The night my son Dike was born, and the nurse placed him in my arms, I looked into his piercing brown eyes and had an instant dislike, almost to the point of hate, overcame me. Was it because he waited so long to make his appearance? According to when he was conceived, he should have been born December 3rd. It was February 4th when he arrived, weighing 15 pounds. The doctor who delivered him said, "Children make their appearance when they are ready," so he would not induce labor.

What's wrong with me? I questioned over the years as my dislike for Dike continued. I read books in psychology and prayed for an answer. I was too ashamed to tell anyone or seek counseling. During the 1940s, going to a 'shrink' meant you must be crazy.

Dike was our second child. Our firstborn was a daughter. Two years after the birth of Dike, we had a third child, a son. I enjoyed my role as a mother and loved my daughter and youngest son. I deliberately forced myself to tolerate Dike. The nagging question of why I did not outgrow or overcome my negative attitude towards him continued to haunt me. No amount of rationalizing or analyzing helped.

In 1965, when Dike turned nineteen, I became interested in hypnosis, self-awareness, and ESP. My husband shared this interest. We began taking courses on these topics. One of the

149

classes was on past-life recall. The instructor, a youthful fifty with light blue eyes and a boyish grin, believed that every thought and impulse in the world is recorded in the Akashic Records.

It is believed by many that the Akashic Hall of Records is in another dimension. Everyone in the world is on file. Their actions, thoughts, words, and experiences are all on record. When one does a past life recall, the information is obtained from these records.

"It is like consulting a reference library," he explained. To give us a demonstration, he asked for a volunteer. Using the hypnotic relaxation approach, he directed the volunteer to close his eyes and relax.

"Now shut out all outward impressions from the mind and begin concentrating upon inner vision." Next, he directed the volunteer to select a lifetime that was in some way connected to his present lifetime. "Perhaps you have a fear, hate, anger, pain, or any strong emotion that you can't understand," he prompted.

"I want to know why I am so afraid of the water and drowning. I won't even go fishing with the guys from work," he explained.

After the instructor induced a relaxation technique by slowly counting from ten to one, he suggested that he go into a deeper state.

The volunteer shared his experience. "My fishing boat is being pulled out to sea by a strong wind. The boat is turning over, and I'm trying to hang on, but I'm slipping." He suddenly shrieked as he raised his arms in the air as if trying to swim. "I can't breathe, I can't breathe," he gasped.

"You are only observing. There is no need to experience," the instructor calmly suggested. "I am now going to count from ten to one. At the count of one, you will open your eyes and feel fine."

After the volunteer opened his eyes, he shook his head as if waking from a bad dream.

"His fear of drowning may well have been a carryover from a past traumatic experience," he told us. Two more volunteers were regressed. All three had unresolved emotions that surfaced during their session.

"If an emotional incident stems from a past life, does knowing the cause solve the problem?" I asked.

"Many times it does, but for some, it takes time. I suggest they mentally repeat this phrase when confronted with their fear, anger, or any emotion that they cannot understand. *'This is the past. I refuse to live in the past.'* Gradually the issue will be resolved," he explained.

It took me several days before I got the courage to experiment on my own. My husband had bought me a crystal ball several weeks earlier after we attended a lecture on the phenomena of crystal gazing. I made it a point to sit and look into the ball every morning when I was alone in the house. Some days I thought I saw figures, sometimes writing appeared, and once I thought I heard someone talking, *"WOW! What an imagination,"* was my general reaction. I shared my research project with only my husband.

"It may take more practice, so don't get discouraged," he said.

After almost a week of crystal gazing, something happened that scared the yell out of me. I had just sat down in my favorite chair and put the ball on the lap tray as usual. Before I began to relax and focus, I heard a loud voice say, *"Are you still a doubting Thomas?"*

I honestly thought there was someone in the room. I even got up and looked in the hall, thinking that someone was playing a joke on me.

"This isn't working for me. Perhaps I'm doing something wrong," I told myself. I went to look for the card of the psychic who had given the lecture on crystal gazing. She had said that we could call her if we had any questions. I told her about my experience and asked if she had any suggestions.

"You may have a block or fear that is preventing you from getting your answers. Trust me; anyone can get answers by crystal gazing. It may take a little more practice for some, but I have never had a student that was not successful," she encouraged. "You <u>are</u> asking the ball a question, aren't you? If you don't, all sorts of bits and pieces of disjointed scenes appear," she told me.

"I have not been asking questions. I just assumed pictures would start coming," I sheepishly confessed.

The next morning I was prepared. The first question on my list was obvious: Why did I have such a dislike for Dike? To my amazement, the ball began to cloud. The next instant, pictures began appearing. The only way I can describe what happened next was as if I was pulled into a scene.

I was there playing a role. I was in an encampment near a battlefield. Somehow, I knew it was taking place in Russia. As the scenario unfolded, I knew I was a boy of fourteen charged with the responsibility of tending to the fire, food, and horses when the men came into camp to rest. There was a continuous whistling howl as the wind whipped through the encampment on the side of the mountain. The only shelter, which could have been a bear's abode at one time, was a small cave three feet tall and perhaps five feet in depth. I would crawl into it every opportunity I had to get out of the biting cold.

The next scene began with a horse and rider entering the camp. I knew it was the captain, and I always dreaded his return. He was cruel and disliked by the men that served under him. Demanding something to eat, he ordered me to take off his boots.

As he was sitting on a log chewing on bread and meat, I began struggling to remove the fur-lined otter boots from his swollen legs. Suddenly, the boot was free, and I slipped backward, causing the boot to fly out of my hands into a puddle of muddy water. Bending to retrieve the boot, to shake the water out before the captain noticed, I felt a sharp burning jab in my side. The captain was kicking me and shouting obscenities. The pain was excruciating, but I managed to escape by running into the cave and crawling as far onto the back as I could.

I crouched into a fetal position as my mouth began filling with warm blood. I had difficulty breathing as light-headedness engulfed me. I knew I must have been dying. With my strength slipping fast, I uttered the same obscenities that the captain had hurled at me. My last words were, *"I hate you…I hate you!"*

A sense of blessed peace overcame me, and all the fear, hate, and agony ended as the picture faded from the ball.

The scenario may have lasted for a heartbeat, an hour, or a year. It was timeless. Then just as abruptly, I became aware of myself back in the room amid familiar surroundings. I knew the captain in that life was my son Dike in this life. To deny my feelings was useless. I was there. I was the boy. I actually heard the wind and felt the cold bite. I felt the kicking. I spent the rest of the morning logging the details of the experience in my journal.

When my husband came home from work that evening, he asked with his usual greeting, "And what exciting thing happened today?"

"You will never believe it," I answered.

"Try me," he encouraged. As we sat in the den, I began sharing the crystal ball experience. He listened with interest, and when I finished, all he said was, "Everything is possible."

Dike was living at home and attending a local college at the time. When he came home that evening, my husband got up, grabbed hold of him, whiled him around, and playfully kicked him in the backside with his knee.

"What did I do to bring that on?" Dike questioned.

"That was for kicking your mother to death many lifetimes ago when you were a captain in the Russian army. She was only fourteen… you bully." He grinned as he waved his hand in a gesture of dismissal.

"Well, if it makes her feel better, I'll try to understand." Dike shrugged his shoulders, and with a trace of forced laughter, he walked towards his room. I decided not to go into details of what brought this all about. He was already referring to me as 'The Great Mystic' after finding out that I had a crystal ball and was experimenting with it.

After that episode, my feelings towards Dike changed. Even if this had happened, so what? That was many lifetimes ago, and we are living in the NOW.

It was several days later when one of my friends called to share a THOUGHT FOR THE DAY that she read in one of her magazines. Although I had never mentioned to anyone but my husband about

153

my experimenting with the crystal ball, the proverb was oddly appropriate.

Yesterday is History
Tomorrow is a Mystery
Today is your Gift
That's why it's called the Present

Coincidence—Happenstance

In 1973, an opportunity presented itself that made it possible for me to get confirmation of the scene I saw in the crystal ball eight years earlier.

I had just returned from England, where I was doing research in séance rooms to determine the difference between thought forms and apparitions. While stopping over in New York, I called a friend who sponsored me when I was on the lecture circuit. I told her about my research, and she suggested I get on a radio talk show. She made the arrangements, and I was able to do the interview from my home in Texas.

A person from the Parapsychology Foundation in New York heard the show. I was contacted and asked to present a paper on my research at the First Psychotronic Congress that would take place in Czechoslovakia. I accepted.

NOTE: The Parapsychology Foundation still exists and can be found at https://parapsychology.org/

Our first stop was Prague, where we met our hosts and colleagues. Our next stop was Leningrad, then on to Moscow. The two weeks spent among the doctors, scientists, and fellow researchers in metaphysics was one of the many highlights I have been privileged to experience.

Before leaving for home, we had a free afternoon to visit some of the palaces that had been converted into museums. I was impressed with the details used to display the periods from Russian history.

There was so much to see, and our guide was hurriedly explaining the displays in the front section of the museum. It was almost closing time when I decided to take off on my own for the rest of the time.

My instinct led me straight to a glass encasement on the far end of the museum. The display held the life-sized figure of a Russian soldier seated on a log. Lying at his side was a pair of otter-lined boots. His piercing brown eyes locked into mine. His pockmarked face, ruddy complexion, and stocky build shocked me. It was my son sitting on the log, exactly as he looks today.

Amazement siphoned the blood from my head as I grasped the rail used to guard the display.

"My God!" I muttered. This was the identical scene that had appeared in my crystal ball eight years earlier.

Why did it take so long for me to finally get my answer to the question, why I didn't like my son?

It took me a long time to accept the fact that planet earth is a classroom of learning, experiencing, overcoming, and understanding. Also, that being incarnated was a way of learning that that is our destiny.

I wanted personal PROOF. I affirm that it was no accident or happenstance that I was invited to Russia to find the proof I needed. Today my big attitude is… so that happened in the past… BIG DEAL. I refuse to live in the past. Forgiveness is a lesson many of us still need to understand. Today, I can truthfully say I learned this lesson, and I am most grateful for all the help I received along the way.

CONFESSIONS OF AN 83-YEAR-OLD SAGE

AND JUST WHO AM I?

ALL ARE CHOSEN; FEW CARE

TO ANSWER THE CALL

Recently I had a question asked me. That I feel needs to be addressed: WHO ARE YOU?

Saving the world is not my assignment. Unlike Sylvia Browne, the dead and I do not converse. Jean Dixon made predictions. I do not.

I am told that I am simply a channel to help people help themselves. That is my mission in this lifetime. I am given assignments by 'messengers' from other dimensions that appear to me in physical form and communicate telepathically. Very rarely do the same messengers appear for each person—which leads me to believe that they are that individual's personal guide or guardian angel.

My assignments do not occur on a daily basis. In fact, they happen so sporadically; I still get startled when a messenger does appear.

But I'm no longer frightened. When their visits first began, I would yell out loud, "Go away! Leave me alone! I must be going crazy." It was a number of years before I realized why they were coming. Yes, I got messages and explanations and dreams and the meditative state, but I was reluctant to acknowledge their presence. It took a lot of patience and convincing on their part before I finally felt safe and confident enough to pursue an assignment.

Today, when a fourth-dimensional messenger appears, I listen to their request, and I wait for three signs (my way of confirmation). I am never foolhardy enough to pick up and move or blurt out something that may only confuse people. '

There are many ways of helping and healing people in the physical, emotional, and spiritual realms. I realize that a doctor practicing traditional medicine is necessary when one develops chemistry imbalances, or their skills are required more repairing the body after an accident. Psychologists and counselors also serve a purpose by listening and offering suggestions when a person is going through mental trauma. Ministers, rabbis, and priests are available when one has doubts and questions about spiritual matters.

I heal with WORDS. The knowledge I convey does not come from books or from college instruction. I simply repeat what is given to me telepathically by another dimensional messenger who is present in the current meeting.

If a person is surprised by the solutions that are offered and asks me if I'm psychic, my usual answer is, "This is one of my days when I am good at guessing." I find no need to describe the messenger that usually accompanies them when we meet. However, not all people have a messenger accompanying them. When this occurs, I engage in small talk such as discussing family and current events, etc.

At age eighty-two, I am enjoying my freedom, space, and love being alone on my five acres and rural Alvarado, Texas. If I have the need for social contact, I let it be known that I'm available. It's a technique I've used for the past thirty-five years. To my guardian, I request, "Let me be a channel to help people help themselves." It doesn't take long before the phone rings, or the letter arrives with a request from a person who is looking for a place to regroup and relax or to simply come to the Center to talk over their challenges.

Yes, I feel fortunate that I'm aware of other dimensions. Our three-dimensional world is our physical classroom for learning life's lessons. The fourth and other dimensions, the unseen worlds, are the site of our counselors and guardian angels—those messengers who offer us guidance and assistance.

There are a number of people in today's society who are aware and operate inter-dimensionally. I feel blessed when we make contact with each other.

But 'Chosen One?' Nope. Like each of us, I know I agreed to the role that I am playing before I came to the physical body and that my own guardians assist me in helping others.

To the many students and friends I have met during this lifetime, I feel I need to make this apology. Forgive me if I worry too much, I am too concerned with your welfare and many times give you suggestions you didn't ask for. I'm an OLD SAGE—I can't help it.

Before bringing my confessions to a close, I have one more suggestion that needs to be conveyed.

MAKE EVERY DAY SPECIAL
Share a joke, hum a song.
Pass some special joy along.
And if someone should come your way
Who doesn't share your joy today…
THE HELL WITH 'EM!

AFTERWORD

I hope this book gave you a glimpse into Helene Hadsell's extraordinary life, making you feel as if you were sitting beside her, having breakfast, and listening to her regale you with tales of her escapades.

Helene wanted to impart the joy and marvel that can be found in every moment, even with life's ups and downs, which is why she wrote these stories down. She knew that writing this book would allow what she learned on her life's journey to be passed on to future generations.

From reminiscing about her travels around the world to Helene's connections with her spirit guides, she touched countless lives with her wit, wisdom, and unique teaching style, including mine. Helene changed my life in immeasurable ways. I hope that you reading her adventures alters the course of your life for the better too.

One adventure after another is what life is all about.
Helene Hadsell

RECOMMENDED READING

Some of the books Helene mentions are now out of print but no less valuable. Be sure to scour used book stores, thrift shops, and flea markets for old copies.

HELENE'S MENTIONS

The Silva Mind Control Method
by José Silva

Helene was not only friends with José Silva for over 30 years, but at one point, she was his Assistant and PR Manager. If you have any trouble mastering Select It, Project It, Expect It, Collect It (SPEC), a manifesting method Helene teaches in her first book, *The Name It & Claim It Game*, you must read José's book as his teachings are what SPEC is derived from, although clearly, Helene put her own spin on it.

You're Not Old Until You're 90
by Rebecca Lattimer

Helene recommends this book in the *Reflections* chapter as Rebecca also had a doctor from another dimension help her heal.

Beyond Biofeedback
by Elmer & Alyce Green

After reading this book, Helene discovered the hand warming technique she had used intuitively was recommended by brain researchers Elmer and Alyce Green to benefit the body.

Predecessors to Dr. Joe Dispenza, and others, the Green's outline the importance of what brain-wave self-regulation can do. *"Theta training is a form of accelerated meditation—and the benefits to its users are incalculable."*

Heal Your Body
by Louise Hay

Similar to Helene, Louise healed herself. Her experience was so profound; not only did she write this book, along with many others, Louise founded a publishing firm, Hay House. This book is a fantastic introduction to the mind-body-spirit connection.

The Power of Positive Thinking
by Norman Vincent Peale

Helene recommended people to this book as a starting point to change their thought patterns. It was through Norman that Helene met Dr. Joesph Murphy, but Helene didn't include any adventures or stories with Norman in any of her books, so I have no details on how or when they met.

You Are Not The Target
by Laura Huxley

This is the book that inspired Helene to add dirty dancing to her repertoire of energy work to dispel negative emotions and mental blocks from her body.

In My Soul I Am Free
by Brad Steiger

Brad wrote Paul Twitchell's biography along with over 100 of his own works. Helene connected with Brad frequently as they both spoke at many of the same events.

The Tiger's Fang
by Paul Twitchell

Helene was lucky enough to also spend time with Paul Twitchell. He uncharacteristically came to her home for a social visit the evening before he lectured. They clearly had a soul contract. He taught her about many of the subjects you read about in this book.

The Power of the Subconscious Mind
by Dr. Joseph Murphy

Not only was Helene friends with José Silva, but she was also friends with Dr. Joseph Murphy. As Helene stated, it's good to repeat the same lessons several times to solidify them in your mind. It is also good to hear similar lessons from different teachers. Sometimes hearing the same concept presented from a slightly different angle helps you more fully grasp the idea.

The Living Brain
by W. Grey Walter

Breakthroughs to Creativity
by Shafica Karagulla

Helene specifically mentions these two books she received from José for her to read as he found them interesting, wanting to share his newfound wisdom along with discussing the thoughts, concepts, and ideas in each.

Thinking and Destiny
by Harold Percival

This is a shift away from the types of books Helene usually mentions, as you may feel it's a 'heavy' read. It's also focused on thinking versus spirituality.

NOTE: Helene mastered reading tarot cards and her crystal ball. She learned from teachers directly and did not mention any resources for others to read. I have not mastered either metaphysical modality; therefore, I am not able to make any recommendations either. However, I do recommend you do your own research, follow your inner voice, and learn from the teachers you resonate with.

CAROLYN'S RECOMMENDS

Sacred Contracts
by Caroline Myss

We all come into this world with a soul contract. This book helps you learn more about your life purpose and identify the spiritual energies that help you discover the lessons you came to 'Earth School' to experience.

Transforming Fate into Destiny
by Robert Ohotto

In life, like cards, the hand we are dealt is our Fate. How we play that hand is our Destiny. Robert teaches you how to identify and heal unconscious blocks that may be obstructing your highest good.

Robert's teachings changed my life in numerous and profound ways. He is the first teacher I recommend if you are seeking an exceptional guide as you grow on your spiritual path.

Ask Your Guides
by Sonia Choquette

Helene spoke a lot about her guides, and this book will help you learn how to connect with yours to nurture your soul and make your time on Earth an adventure precisely as Helene wished for all her students.

The Spontaneous Fulfillment of Desire
by Deepak Chopra

There are no coincidences. For example, it wasn't a coincidence I learned about Helene and read her book(s) but also spent four days with her as well. It set up the opportunity for me to eventually share her work.

In his book, you will discover how we are all connected to everything that exists and everything that is yet to come. The more aware you become and connect to the field of infinite possibilities, the more 'coincidences' you experience.

Becoming Supernatural
by Dr. Joe Dispenza

Joe teaches you, through various meditations, how to tune into Universal energies, tap into other realms, and create the life you desire.

As each teacher stands on the shoulders of their predecessors, Joe takes biofeedback, meditating and stepping into the unknown to a new level.

What the Bleep Do You Know?
DVD

This documentary examines the connection between quantum physics and consciousness. Using a story format, it follows the heroine on her journey, and along the way, we discover where science and spirituality converge.

Finding Joe
DVD

This is a documentary about Joseph Campbell. He was famous for teaching that each of us is on A Hero's Journey, comparing our life experiences/patterns with mythology and cultural stories.

NOTE: If you want to read more of my favorites, you can find a more comprehensive list on my website:
http://bit.ly/CarolynsFavoriteBooks

AUTHORS

HELENE HADSELL

Helene Hadsell was proof not only of her dynamic philosophy of life, but her practice of positive thinking in the energetic pursuit of her goals has brought her rich rewards in terms of spiritual, physical, and material well-being. This book is her true account of the amazing events of her life that bear out her conviction that anyone can achieve anything their mind can conceive if they firmly resolve to do so.

In 1986 she founded Delta Sciences as a retreat center and had people come from all over the world - England, Switzerland, Hungary, Peru, as well as people from every state in the USA.

Helene Hadsell was the mother of three children, Chris, Dike, and Pamela, three grandchildren, and three great-grandchildren. She lived in Alverado, Texas, with her husband Pat, who shared her interest in helping people improve their lives through mental power.

CAROLYN WILMAN

Carolyn Wilman (aka @IdeaMajesty) is a Digital Marketer that works with companies to create and viral market winning promotions and programs, maximizing their ROI and loyal customers.

Her efforts as a marketing expert landed her on the cover of Marketing Magazine, was named by MORE Magazine as one of Canada's Top 40 Women over 40, and featured in High Stakes Sweepers, a pilot for TLC.

Ms. Wilman is also the author of two best-selling books on finding, organizing, entering, and winning sweepstakes, along with re-releasing Helene's first book, *The Name It & Claim It Game*.

Carolyn is a single mother of one who resides in Oshawa, Ontario, who believes her purpose in life is to teach others how to have more fun and embrace the grand adventure we call LIFE.

The three things
that make life
worthwhile:
To feel useful by
doing something;
To be loved by
someone; and
To have something
to look forward to.
Helene Hadsell